COLLECTOR'S ENCYCLOPEDIA OF

MADAME ALEXANDER DOLLS

1948 – 1965

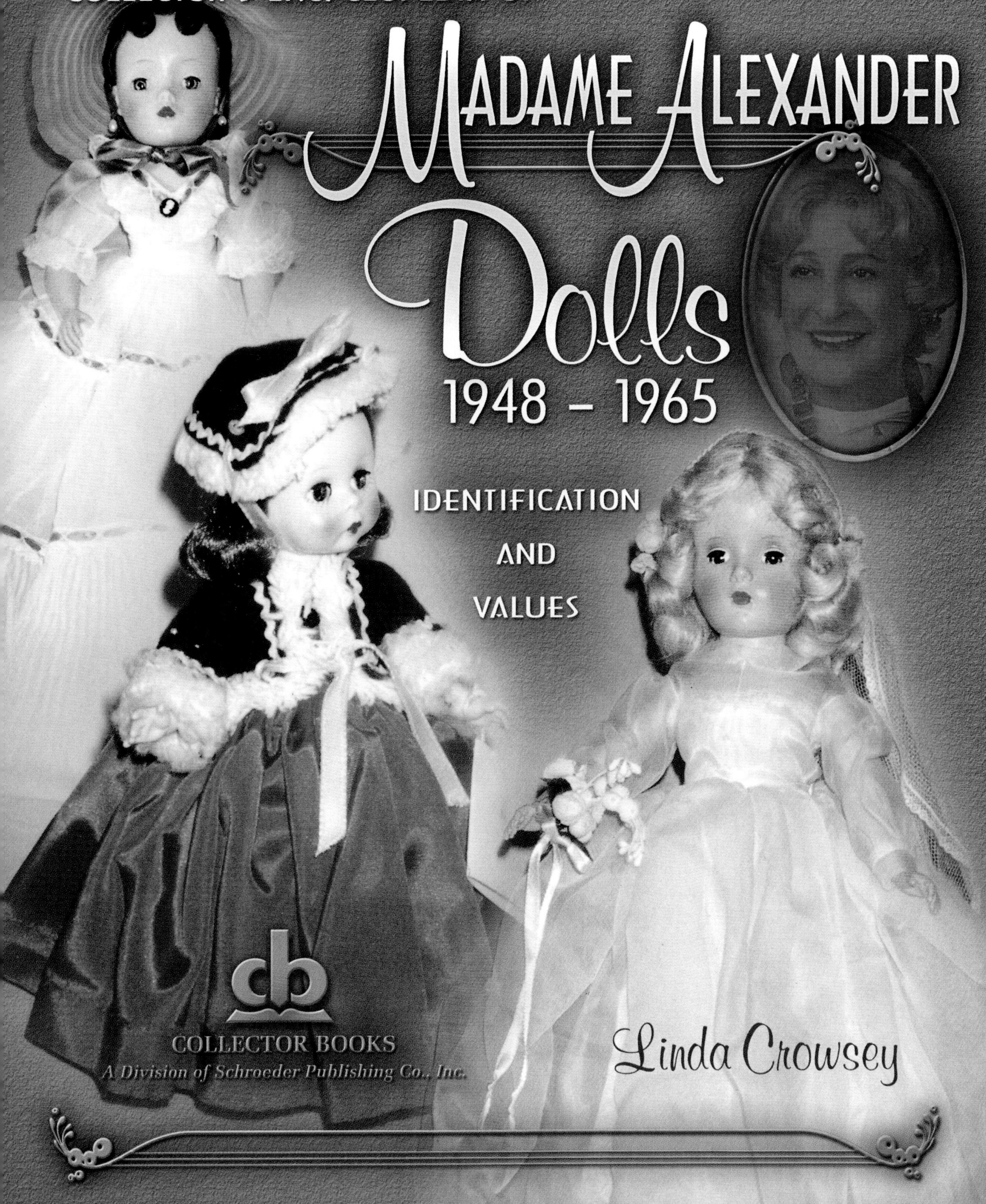

IDENTIFICATION AND VALUES

Linda Crowsey

COLLECTOR BOOKS
A Division of Schroeder Publishing Co., Inc.

Front Cover:
Top left — 20" Scarlett Portrait Cissy, 1961, $1,500.00+.
Lower left — 8" Mary Louise, 1954, $1,500.00+.
Lower right — 14" Peggy Bride, 1950, $1,000.00+.

Back Cover:
Left — 12" Lissy, 1956 – 1958, $850.00.
Middle — 10" Cissette, 1957, $850.00.
Right — 8" Queen Elizabeth, 1954, $1,200.00+.

Cover design by Beth Summers
Book design by Marty Turner

COLLECTOR BOOKS
P.O. Box 3009
Paducah, KY 42002-3009

www.collectorbooks.com

The current values in this book should be used only as a guide. They are not intended to set prices, which vary from one section of the country to another. Auction prices as well as dealer prices vary greatly and are affected by condition as well as demand. Neither the author nor the publisher assumes responsibility for any losses that might be incurred as a result of consulting this guide.

Contents

In Memorium

You will live on in our memories through your books, research, and love of dolls that you shared with everyone you met.

Patricia R. Smith

2003

Dedication

This book is dedicated to Madame Beatrice Alexander and to Gale Jarvis. Madame Alexander set the standard in the doll world for making the most beautiful dolls out of the finest materials available. Today, Gale Jarvis, president of the Alexander Doll Company, continues this tradition of making top quality beautiful award-winning dolls that collectors cherish.

Acknowledgments

My sincere thanks to the following for sharing their dolls in this book. Brooklyn Children's Museum Curator Nancy Paine, Gary Green, Susan Huey, Kathryn LaBounty, Lahanta McIntyre, Christene McWilliams, Marge Meisinger, Florence Phelps, Ric Markin, Dwight Smith, Marylee Stallings, Mike Way, and Susan York. Very special thanks to Terri Queen, Ann McCurdy, Ben and Helen Thomas for their pictures and extraordinary help with this book.

Pricing

The prices contained in this section range from all original dolls that may be missing small items such as original shoes, items in the hand, jewelry, gloves etc. in good condition but may have shelf dust or very minor damage to the very pristine "take your breath away" mint dolls. It is very important that collectors keep in mind that these prices are to be used as a guide and a starting point to determine the price of a doll. Condition is critical in determining the value of a doll. The vast majority of dolls in this book are mint. I have noted where dolls are not complete.

The Madame Alexander Doll Company

The Alexander Doll Company began in 1923 when Madame Beatrice Alexander joined with her husband, Phillip Behrman, to form the company. Beatrice Alexander was born March 9, 1895, in Brooklyn, New York. Her father, Maurice Alexander, owned the first doll hospital in America. He repaired antiques and restored porcelain and bisque dolls. Young Beatrice often saw how upset children were when their favorite doll was broken. Some of Madame's earliest dolls were made of cloth which did not break when dropped.

The Alexander Company was making quality composition dolls in the 1930s. These dolls were not easily broken and costumes were designed for the dolls that were of the finest materials. The Alexander Company survived during difficult economic times due to Madame's creativity and her unyielding desire to make breathtakingly beautiful dolls.

A huge change was made in the Alexander Doll Company in 1948 when the factory began making dolls of hard plastic instead of composition. Madame Alexander was awarded the Fashion Academy Gold Medal in 1951, 1952, 1953, and 1954 for the fashions that were designed for her dolls. Many collectors often refer to the 1950s as the "golden era" of the Alexander Doll Company. During this time Cissy, Cissette, and 8" Wendy were designed and are a major part of the Alexander Company line today. The Glamour Girls, Beaux Arts, Me and My Shadow dolls, as well as the Coronation Set and the extremely rare Bible Characters were made. There was an almost endless variety of dolls made in the 1950s in different sizes with wardrobes for every occasion. The dolls made during the 1948 to 1965 period are some of the most sought after of all dolls. "A Child's Dream Come True" was the caption a 1956 Alexander catalog. There can be no doubt adults as well as children have dreamed of Alexander dolls!

Madame Alexander sold the Alexander Doll Company to private investors in 1988. The Alexander Company celebrated its eightieth anniversary in 2003. The Alexander Company is located at the same location in New York City since the 1950s. The showroom of the current Alexander line, the Heritage Gallery of vintage Alexanders, the Alexander Doll Hospital, and the factory store are all at the 615 West 131st Street address. Under the leadership of President Gale Jarvis, the Alexander Company continues the legacy of making the highest quality and most beautiful dolls in the world.

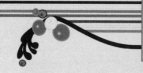

Alexander-kins

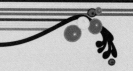

The first year of production was 1953. The dolls were made of hard plastic and were heavier than later 8" dolls. They had straight legs and did not walk. The dolls had "Alex" on their back from 1953 to 1976 when it was changed to "Alexander." Quiz-kins were made in 1953 only. Quiz-kins had two buttons on their back for the head to nod yes or no. Some Quiz-kins as well as Alexander-kins had painted- on hair. In 1953 many of the dolls had molded hair with a glued on wig.

In 1954 and 1955 the dolls were walkers with straight legs attached by a rod to the head which made the head move back and forth when the legs were made to "walk."

From 1956 to 1965 the dolls had joints at the knee that enabled the dolls to sit, kneel, and to be posed in various ways. They were also walkers.

Dolls came dressed in an array of outfits each year. Alexander-kins were also sold as basic dolls wearing panties, shoes, and socks. Boxed outfits were sold separately. Some outfits were sold on dressed dolls as well as in boxed sets. Even characters such as the 1957 Aunt Pitty Pat and Nana the Governess came as dressed dolls and with boxed outfits. Fuzzy sole shoes came on dolls from 1953 until around 1958. The soles are somewhat "fuzzy" to the touch.

Mint-in-box dolls are often found with the wrong boxes. The boxes often only had order numbers on them. Stores would display the dolls and when one was sold the clerk would take a box from the storage area without checking to see if the number corresponded with the number in the booklet or catalog. Numbers for dressed dolls were three digits such as #435 for Aunt Pitty Pat while the boxed outfit the three digits were preceded with a 0 (#0435).

Madame Alexander began production of 8" international dolls in 1961. The dolls were bend knee walkers. Some dolls had the Wendy Ann face and a few had the Maggie Mixup face. The production of 8" international dolls continues today and the names change at times. An example is Italy for Italian or Switzerland for Swiss. The dolls made from 1961 to 1965 as bend knee walkers are Argentine Boy and Girl, Brazil, Spanish Boy and Girl, Dutch Boy and Girl, Mexican, Hungarian, Irish, Russian, Peruvian Boy, Greek Boy, Israeli, Swedish, French, Swiss, Scots Lass, India, Ecuador, Tyrolean Boy and Girl, Bolivia, and Polish.

The following abbreviations are used in the descriptions.

SLNW—straight leg, non-walker
SLW—straight leg walker
BKW—bend knee walker

1953 – 1954
Ballerina, 8", SLW
(Wendy Ann)
Rare cornflower blue tutu
Mint in original box
$800.00 – 1,400.00

1953
Easter, 8", SLNW
(Wendy Ann)
Organdy dress, carrying a
basket with chicken and
small tennis racket
$700.00 – 1,000.00

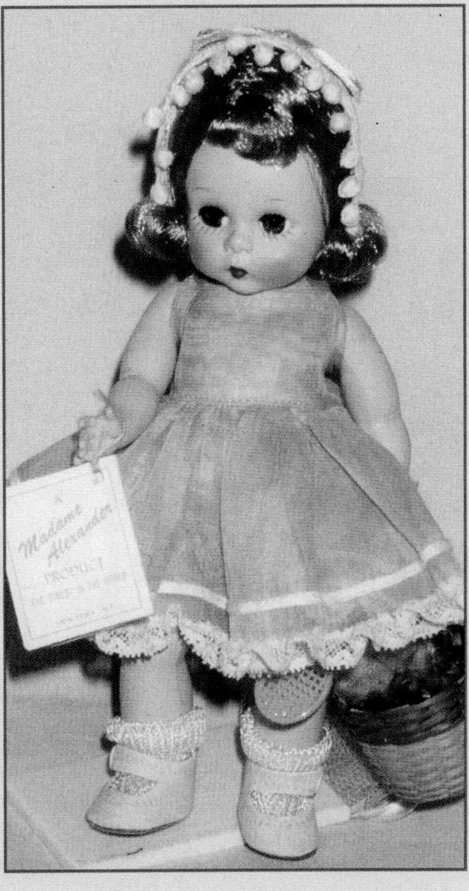

1953
Wendy Ann Bridesmaid, 8", SLNW
(Wendy Ann)
Hard to find in yellow
Mint in box
$750.00 – 1,200.00

1953
Southern Belle, 8", SLNW
(Wendy Ann)
White long cotton gown with two rows of lace, pink silk roses at waist and on hat
$800.00 – 1,300.00

1953
Little Southern Girl, 8", SLNW
(Wendy Ann)
Lace trimmed organdy dress with straw hat
$800.00 – 1,300.00

1953
Wendy, 8", SLNW
(Wendy Ann)
White organdy dress under a pink coat and felt bonnet
Tag: "Alexander-kin"
$600.00 – 950.00

1953
Alexander-kin, 8", SLNW
(Wendy Ann)
Cotton school dress and pinafore
Mint in orginal box
$550.00 – 1,000.00

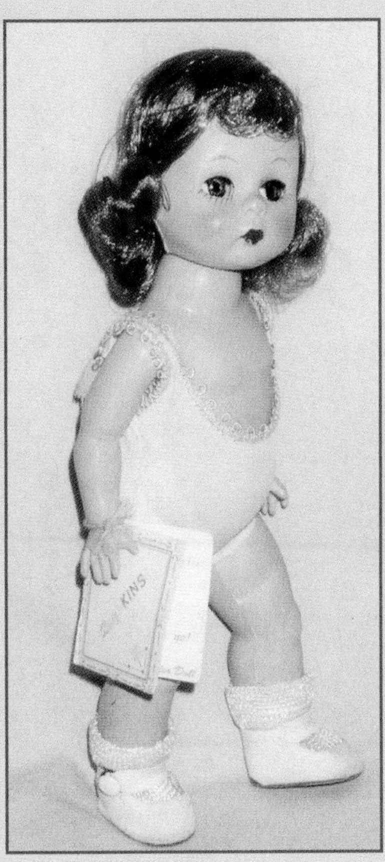

1953
Quiz-kin, 8", SLNW
(Wendy Ann)
Original romper, has yes and no buttons on back of doll
$450.00 – 825.00

1953
Quiz-kin, 8", SLNW
(Wendy Ann)
Original romper, came in various prints
$450.00 – 850.00

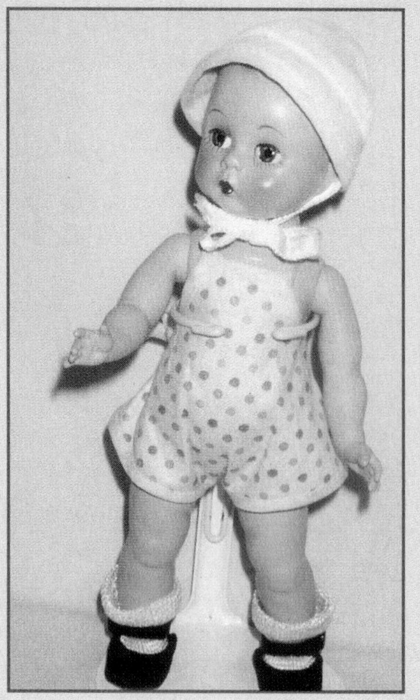

1953
Quiz-kin, 8", SLNW
(Wendy Ann)
Original romper, has yes and no buttons on back
$450.00 – 850.00

1953
Agatha, 8", SLNW
(Wendy Ann)
Polished cotton dress, came in a variety of prints
$900.00 – 1,600.00

1953
Bride Quiz-kin, 8", SLNW
(Wendy Ann)
Satin bodice with tulle skirt
$700.00 – 1,200.00

1953
Quiz-kin Groom, 8", SLNW
(Wendy Ann)
Painted head, all original
$450.00 – 750.00

1953 – 1954
"Little Edwardian," 8", SLNW or SLW
Cotton dress with organdy sleeves
Tag: "Alexander-kin"
$850.00 – 1,500.00

1953 – 1954
"Little Madaline," 8", SLNW
(Wendy Ann)
All original
Tag: "Alexander-kin"
$900.00 – 1,600.00

1953 – 1954
"Apple Annie of Broadway," 8", SLNW
(Wendy Ann)
Plaid dress and straw hat
$800.00 – 1,300.00

1953 – 1954
8", SLNW
(Wendy Ann)
Jumper outfit with one piece bloomers attached to organdy blouse under the jumper, original starched lace hat, buttons down back
$475.00 – 900.00

1954 Bible Characters

In 1954 eight Bible Characters were made and are considered to be the rarest of the 8" dolls made by Madame Alexander. The Bible Characters were made in extremely limited numbers and no information has surfaced to know exactly how many were made. The eight dolls appeared in a black and white Herald House advertisement in 1954. There had been doubt whether Queen Esther and Mary of Bethany had ever been put into production until this set surfaced. Rhoda and Timothy had only been seen as prototypes.

The Bible Characters pictured are all straight leg walkers. A few of the Bible Characters are known to be straight leg nonwalkers. This set was found in the original boxes. All have black eyes with no pupils except for Queen Esther who has dark brown eyes with no pupils. Bible characters, $4,500.00 – 10,000.00 each.

1954 Bible Character
Joseph, 8", SLW
Coat of many colors made of felt with felt scallops, a blue undergarment with a leather skirt that ties on the shoulder, deep red leather belt

1954 Bible Character
Rhoda, 8", SLW
Striped linen dress, felt hat with covered gold buttons over ears, carries a gold lantern, dark brown flip style hairdo

1954 Bible Character
Queen Esther, 8", SLW
Taffeta undergarment trimmed in gold, robe of purple taffeta and gold leaf on white taffeta, gold crown with purple scarf
Original box

1954 Bible Character
Martha, 8", SLW
Red cotton dress trimmed with picot, headpiece of red and white flower trim on navy band, Star of David in the center, blue scarf attached

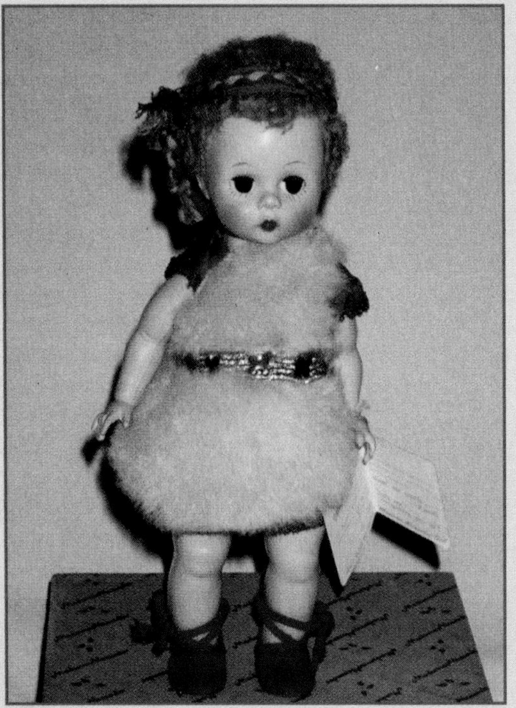

1954 Bible Character
David, 8", SLW
Faux fur tied at the shoulder, gold elastic belt snaps in back and is decorated with x brads, green undergarment

1954 Bible Character
Mary of Bethany, 8", SLW
Polished cotton dress with green overdress, green organdy headpiece attached by black elastic

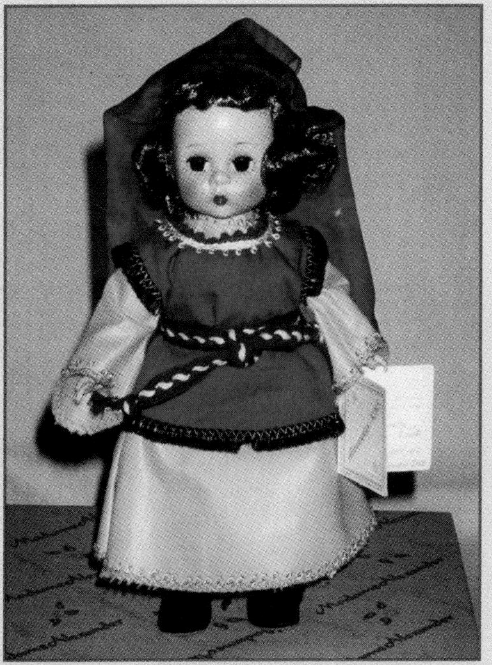

1954 Bible Character
Ruth, 8", SLW
Navy blue dress with picot trim and tied with red, yellow, and green braid, scarf is attached to a gold band with stars

1954 Bible Character
Timothy, 8", SLW
Brown linen outfit is trimmed with braid and fringe, one-piece Star of David on the back of felt hat

1954
#2030C, Victoria, 8"
Me and My Shadow Series
Matches 18" doll
Blue taffeta dress
Mint in box
$1,3000.00 – 2,400.00

1954
"Mary Louise," 8", SLW
(Wendy Ann)
Me and My Shadow Series
Godey period costume
$1,500.00 – 2,400.00

1954
Rainy Day, 8", SLW
(Wendy Ann)
Striped taffeta raincoat set
$350.00 – 700.00

1954
#0030A, Queen Elizabeth, 8", SLW
(Wendy Ann)
Me and My Shadow Series
Brocade court gown, purple
velvet robe
Tag: "Alexander-kins"
$1,200.00 – 2,000.00

1954
Beth of Little Women, 8", SLW
(Wendy Ann)
Cotton dress, bow on sleeve
matches bow in hair
$400.00 – 850.00

1954
#365, Alice in Wonderland, 8", SLW
(Wendy Ann)
Cotton dress with sheer nylon pinafore
$425.00 – 850.00

1954
Little Madeline, 8", SLW
(Wendy Ann)
Special hairdo, denim pants attached to a red stripe top, denim jacket
$550.00 – 950.00

1954
#480, Guardian Angel, 8", BKW
(Wendy Ann)
Multi-layered white wings, gold halo attached to clear plastic gold harp
$700.00 – 1,400.00

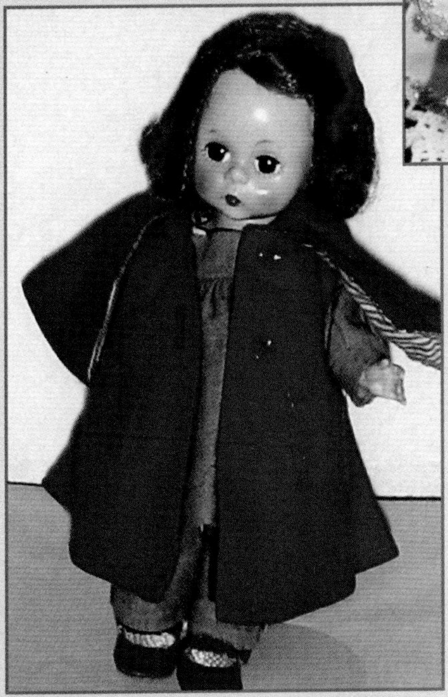

1954
Little Madeline, 8", SLW
(Wendy Ann)
Red Sherlock Holmes type coat
Tag: "Madeline"
Coat only $95.00

1954
#388, Wendy, 8", SLW
(Wendy Ann)
Pleated dress with felt coat and hat
$500.00 – 900.00

1954
Day in the Country, 8", SLW
(Wendy Ann)
Pink bodice, striped skirt, and
straw hat with flowers
$750.00 – 1,400.00

1954
Maypole Dance, 8", SLW
(Wendy Ann)
Organdy dress and pinafore
$450.00 – 950.00

1954
Little Victoria, 8", BKW
(Wendy Ann)
Striped cotton dress with velvet bodice, matches 15", 18", 25" dolls made in 1954
$900.00 – 1,500.00

1954
Alexander-kin, 8", SLW
(Wendy Ann)
Pink taffeta jumper and hat
$375.00 – 750.00

1954
Southern Belle, 8", SLW
(Wendy Ann)
Delicate organdy and lace dress
$850.00 – 1,400.00

1954
So Dressed Up, 8", SLW
(Wendy Ann)
Navy taffeta dress and hot pink velvet hat
Tag: "Alexander-kins"
$600.00 – 950.00

1955
#458, Maypole Dance, 8", SLW
(Wendy Ann)
Taffeta dress with yoke of
organza, flower circlet
in hair
$450.00 – 850.00

1955
#440, Wendy Plays in Garden, 8", SLW
(Wendy Ann)
Cotton dress, pinafore, and hat, original dog
$475.00 – 900.00

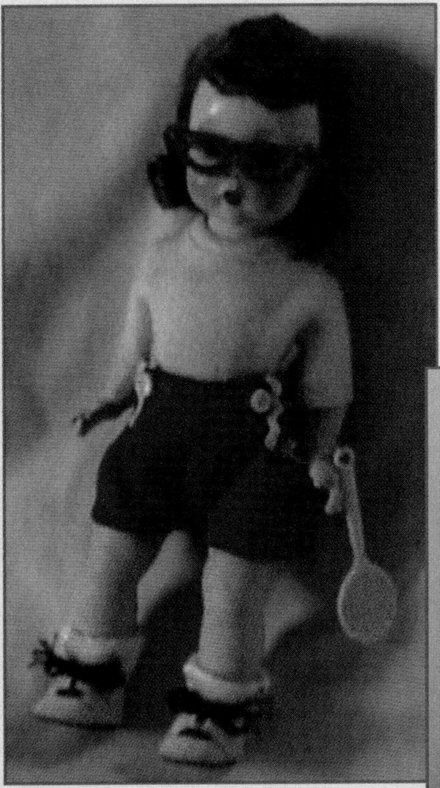

1955
#415, Tennis, 8", SLW
(Wendy Ann)
All original
Tag: "Alexander-kins"
$425.00 – 750.00

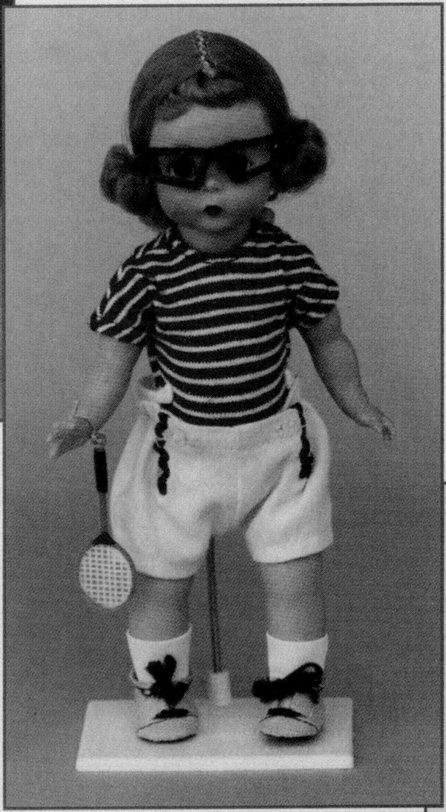

1955
#415, Tennis, 8", SLW
(Wendy Ann)
All original, came in various colors of shirt and pants
$425.00 – 750.00

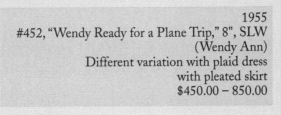

1955
#452, "Wendy Ready for a Plane Trip," 8", SLW
(Wendy Ann)
Different variation with plaid dress with pleated skirt
$450.00 – 850.00

1954 – 1955
Wendy, 8", SLW
(Wendy Ann)
All cotton, came in variety of colors and prints
$375.00 – 700.00

Neiman-Marcus, special doll of 1955
8", 1955
(Wendy)
Came in case, doll also sold separately
Dress tag: "Jane Miller"
$900.00 – 1,700.00

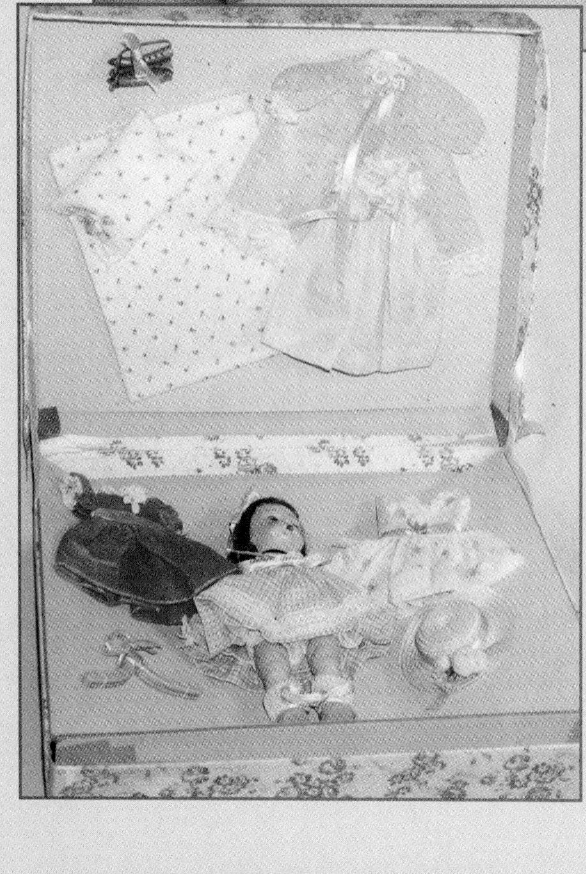

1955
FAO Schwarz store special, 8", SLW
(Wendy Ann)
Clothes tag: "Alexander-kins"
$1,500.00 – 2,500.00

1955
Wendy, 8", SLW
(Wendy Ann)
Basic bra and panties, unusual hairstyle, parted at side and rolled back
$350.00 – 700.00

1955
#457, "Wendy Goes To Sunday School," 8", SLW
(Wendy Ann)
Organdy dress with lace
$425.00 – 850.00

1955
#478, Wendy's Bridesmaid, 8", SLW
(Wendy Ann)
Pink nylon tulle dress and flower cap
$650.00 – 1,000.00

1955
#475, Wendy, 8", SLW
(Wendy Ann)
Heavy satin gown with Juliet cap with tulle attached
$800.00+

1955
#484, Highland Fling, 8", SLW
(Wendy Ann)
Red dress with tartan sash draped across bodice, hat matches sash
$600.00 – 950.00

1955
#485, Scarlett O'Hara, 8", SLW
(Wendy Ann)
Flower muslin trimmed with braid and sleeves of tulle, picture hat
$1,200.00 – 1,800.00

1955
#491, Little Godey Lady, 8", SLW
(Wendy Ann)
Cerise taffeta gown with beaded black wool felt jacket
Tag: "Alexander-kin"
$1,200.00 – 1,800.00

1955
#487, Lady in Waiting, 8", SLW
(Wendy Ann)
Satin dress with coronet veil, rare doll
$1,200.00 – 2,000.00

1955
#492, Cinderella, 8", SLW
(Wendy Ann)
Blue taffeta gown trimmed
in silver, silver tiara
$800.00 – 1,300.00

1955
#442, Wendy, 8", SLW
(Wendy Ann)
Polished cotton dress and pinafore with print pocket
Mint in box
$550.00 – 995.00

1955
Meg of Little Women, 8", SLW
(Wendy Ann)
Checked dress and cotton apron
$275.00 – 475.00

1955
Marme of Little Women, 8", SLW
(Wendy Ann)
Cotton dress taffeta apron
$275.00 – 475.00

1955
Amy of Little Women, 8", SLW
(Wendy Ann)
Polished cotton dress with organdy inset at neck
$300.00 – 500.00

1955
Jo of Little Women, 8", SLW
(Wendy Ann)
Red cotton dress
$275.00 – 475.00

1955
#488, Garden Party, 8", SLW
(Wendy Ann)
Pink organza dress trimmed in lace
$1,200.00 – 2,000.00

1955
#474, Romeo & #473, Juliet, 8", SLW
(Wendy Ann)
Juliet wears a brocade gown and overdress, Romeo wears purple tights, gold boots, and felt jacket
Romeo $700.00 – 1,200.00
Juliet $850.00 – 1,500.00

1955
#471, Red Riding Hood, 8", SLW
(Wendy Ann)
White taffeta dress with red taffeta cape
$500.00 – 1,000.00

1955
#476, Wendy Loves to Waltz, 8", SLW
(Wendy Ann)
Long white organdy dress trimmed with rickrack and red satin bag
$650.00 – 1,350.00

1955
#470, Gretel & #445, Hansel, 8", SLW (Wendy Ann)
Gretel wears pink taffeta dress with cotton pinafore, Hansel wears black velvet pants, white shirt, and striped stockings
$500.00 – 950.00 each

1955
#472, Curly Locks, 8", SLW (Wendy Ann)
Pale yellow taffeta dress with flowered pinafore, lace cap
$700.00 – 1,200.00

1955
#481, Wendy Does the Mambo, 8", SLW (Wendy Ann)
Striped dress with Spanish shawl, gold earrings, and lace fan
$550.00 – 950.00

1955
#499, Queen Elizabeth, 8", SLW
(Wendy Ann)
Court gown of white brocade with red velvet robe
$750.00 – 1,200.00

1955
#489, Bo Peep, 8", SLW
(Wendy Ann)
Mauve taffeta dress with rosebud print panniers
$500.00 – 950.00

1955
#444, Wendy, 8", SLW
Green dress with flowered pinafore,
green hat, and slippers
$375.00 – 850.00

1955
#453, Wendy Likes a Rainy Day, 8", SLW
(Wendy Ann)
Pink raincoat and bonnet, blue polka dot dress, blue boots
$375.00 – 800.00

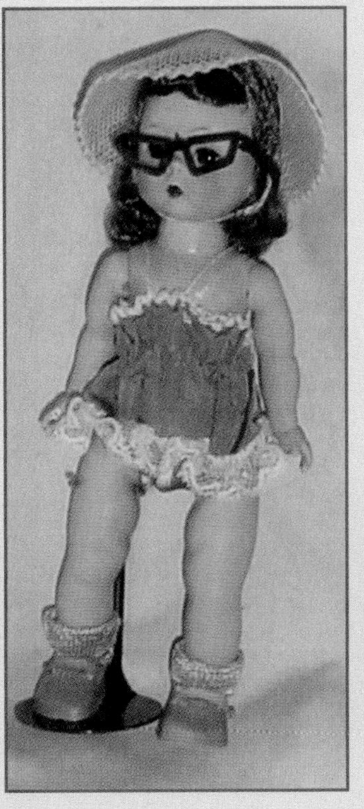

1955
#406, Wendy, 8", SLW
(Wendy Ann)
Lace-trimmed swimsuit, beach hat, and original glasses, shoes not original
$250.00 – 450.00

1955
#456, Wendy Takes Her Dog for a Walk, 8", SLW
(Wendy Ann)
Checked cotton dress, straw hat, original dog
$375.00 – 800.00

1955
#450, "Visitors Day at School," 8", SLW
(Wendy Ann)
Cotton dress with checked pinafore, straw hat with flowers
$350.00 – 750.00

1955
#449, Dude Ranch, 8", SLW
(Wendy Ann)
Denim jeans and checked cotton shirt, straw sombrero hat
$650.00 – 1,000.00

1955
#452, Plane Trip, 8", SLW
(Wendy Ann)
Polished cotton dress with felt jacket and hat
$425.00 – 850.00

1955
#460, Wendy, 8", SLW
(Wendy Ann)
Chartreuse cotton dress with flowered pinafore
$350.00 – 750.00

1955
#461, Best Man, 8", SLW
(Wendy Ann)
One-piece pants and shirt, white jacket
$650.00 – 950.00

1955
#426, "Wendy Goes Roller Skating," 8", SLW
(Wendy Ann)
Taffeta skirt, jersey bodysuit, and felt hat
$400.00 – 900.00

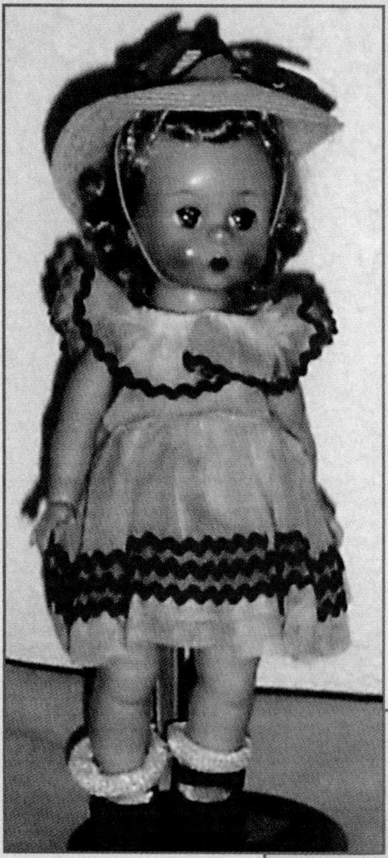

1955
#447, Wendy's Tea Party at Grandma's, 8", SLW
(Wendy Ann)
Organdy dress and straw hat
$375.00 – 800.00

1955
#482, Wendy Drum Majorette, 8", SLW
(Wendy Ann)
All original with baton
$700.00 – 1,250.00

1955
#486, Train Journey, 8", SLW
(Wendy Ann)
Pleated plaid dress with felt jacket and hat
$400.00 – 775.00

1955
#453, Wendy Likes a Rainy Day, 8", SLW
(Wendy Ann)
Polka dot taffeta dress and hat
$375.00 – 800.00

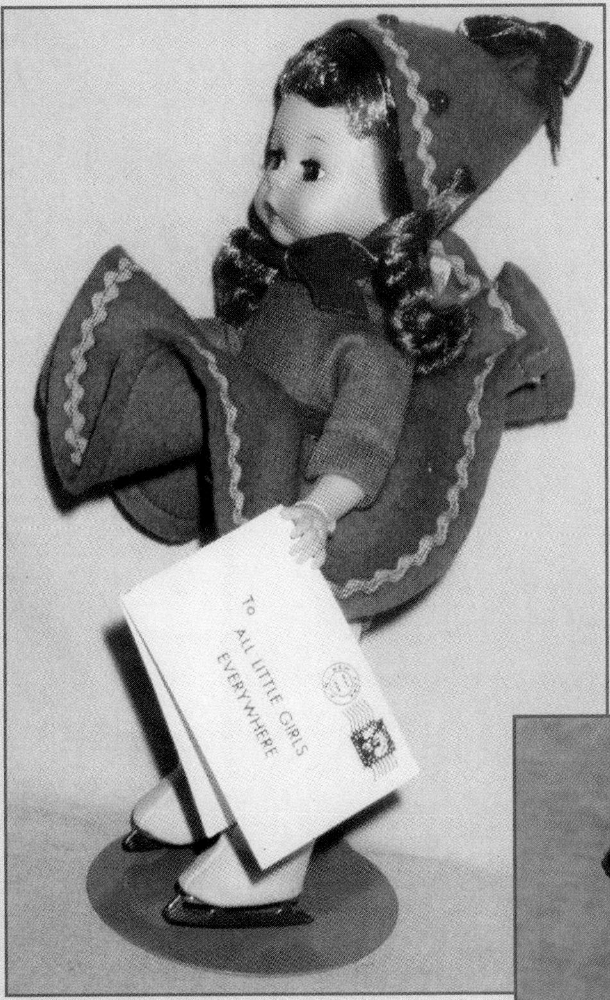

1956
#555, Wendy Goes Ice Skating, 8", BKW
(Wendy Ann)
Felt bonnet and skirt over bodysuit, ice skates came in various colors
$600.00 – 1,000.00

1955
#455, Birthday Party, 8", SLW
(Wendy Ann)
Mauve taffeta with elaborate pinafore trimmed with braid and flowers
$400.00 – 850.00

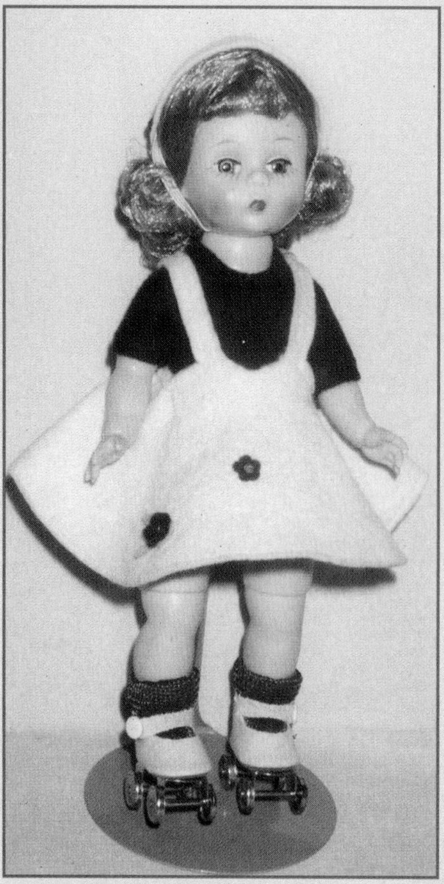

1956
#556, "Wendy Thinks Roller Skating Is Fun," 8", BKW
(Wendy Ann)
Felt jumper with navy bodysuit
$550.00 – 950.00

1956
#555, "Wendy Goes Ice Skating," 8", BKW
(Wendy Ann)
Felt bonnet and skirt over bodysuit
$600.00 – 1,000.00

1956
#585, Hot Morning, 8", BKW
(Wendy Ann)
Polished cotton dress, straw hat with flowers
$450.00 – 850.00

1956
#892, Story Princess, 8", BKW
(Wendy Ann)
Nylon tulle, original crown and wand,
matches Story Princess made in 15" and 18"
$800.00 – 1,700.00

1956
#568, Wendy Runs to Market, 8", BKW
(Wendy Ann)
Cotton dress with pique pinafore and hat
$325.00 – 750.00

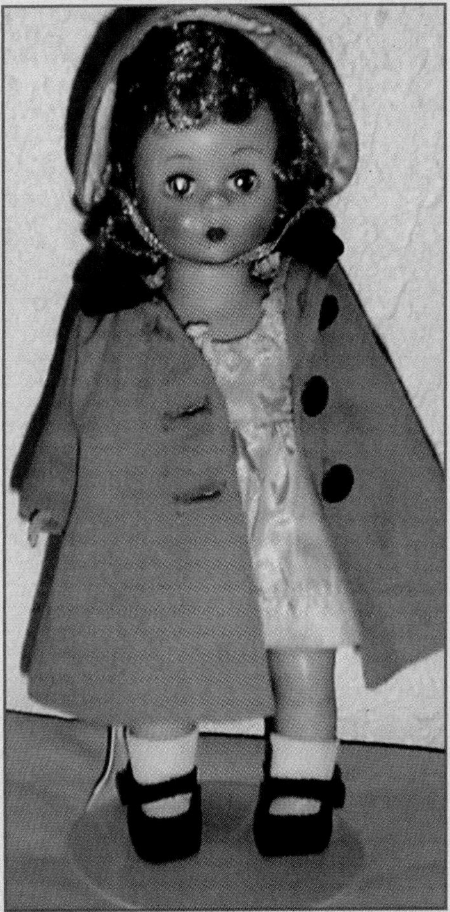

1956
#580, Wendy Needs More than One Coat, 8", BKW
(Wendy Ann)
Gabardine coat and hat over taffeta dress
$375.00 – 800.00

1956
#625, Wendy Wears a Charming Ensemble, 8", BKW (Wendy Ann)
Velvet coat and hat over taffeta dress, original muff
$700.00 – 1,250.00

1956
Amy of Little Women, 8", BKW (Wendy Ann)
Cotton dress with print pinafore
$275.00 – 450.00

1956
#823, Wendy Dressed in a Ballgown, 8", BKW (Wendy Ann)
Taffeta gown with a gold tiara
$900.00 – 1,600.00

1956
#632, Cousin Grace, 8", BKW
(Wendy Ann)
Flowered silk dress and picture hat
$1,500.00 – 2,200.00

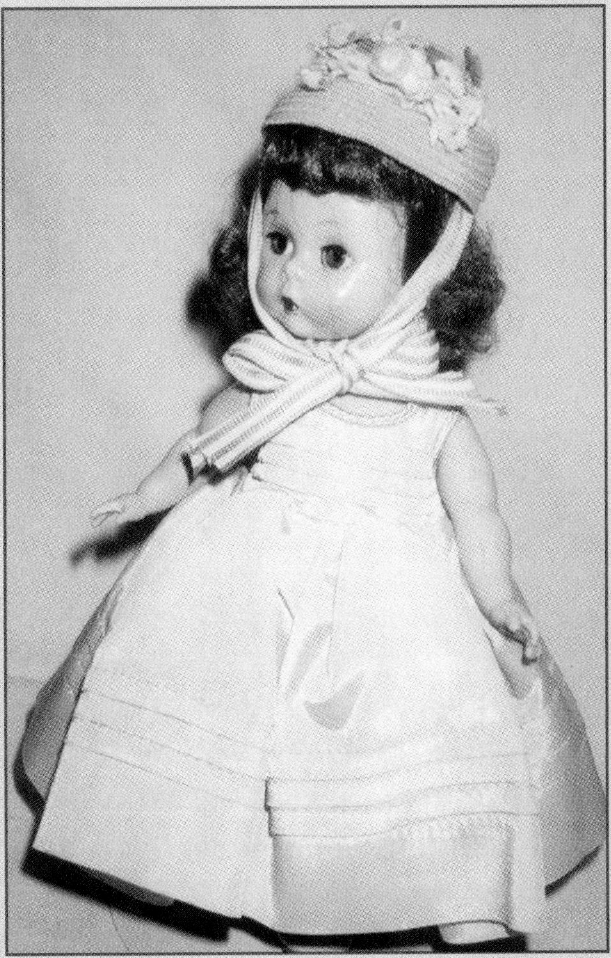

1956
#605, June Wedding, 8", BKW
(Wendy Ann)
Taffeta dress, flower trimmed hat, gold slippers
$900.00 – 1,800.00

1956
#602, Flower Girl, 8", BKW
(Wendy Ann)
Satin gown with circular skirt and pink sash
$700.00 – 1,400.00

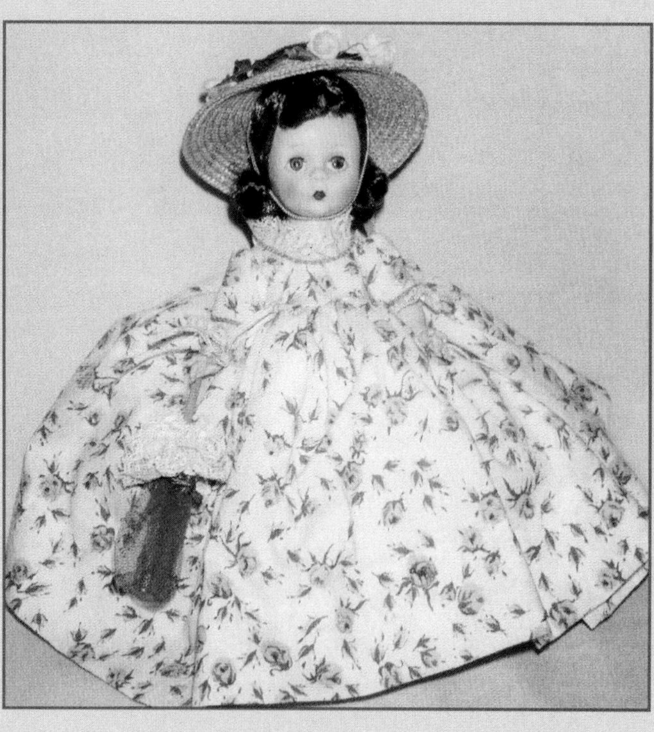

1956
#631, Scarlett, 8", BKW
(Wendy Ann)
Rosebud muslin dress with picture hat
$950.00 – 1,800.00

1956
#630, Cousin Karen, 8", BKW
(Wendy Ann)
Flower cotton dress with velvet bodice
$1,200.00 – 2,000.00

1956
#564, Wendy Loves Ballet Lessons, 8", BKW
(Wendy Ann)
Nylon tulle with satin bodice
$400.00 – 900.00

1956?
Ballerina, 8", BKW
(Wendy Ann)
Satin bodice with green tutu, hard to find, missing headpiece
$550.00 – 950.00

1956
Wendy, 8", BKW
(Wendy Ann)
Coat is the same as 1956 #625,
Wendy Wears a Charming Ensemble
Different hat
$550.00 – 900.00

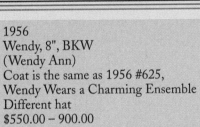

1956
#620, Garden Party, 8", BKW
(Wendy Ann)
Swiss organdy dress and straw hat with
flowers and streamers
$900.00 – 1,600.00

1956
#579, Parlor Maid, 8", BKW
(Wendy Ann)
White organdy apron and cap,
black taffeta dress
$750.00 – 1,250.00

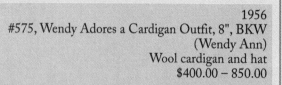

1956
#575, Wendy Adores a Cardigan Outfit, 8", BKW
(Wendy Ann)
Wool cardigan and hat
$400.00 – 850.00

1956
Wendy in Her Window Box gift set,
8", BKW
(Wendy Ann)
FAO Schwarz exclusive
$3,000.00+

1956
#606, Wendy's First Long Dancing Dress, 8", BKW
(Wendy Ann)
White nylon tulle dress with velvet sash
and hair ribbon
$700.00 – 1,200.00

1956
#601, Wendy Goes to the Ballet, 8", BKW
(Wendy Ann)
Green taffeta dress with yoke of pink velvet, missing tulle bandeau
$800.00 – 1,400.00

1956
#616, McGuffey Ana, 8", BKW
(Wendy Ann)
Plaid dress, pinafore, and straw hat
Tag: "Alexander-kins"
$650.00 – 1,150.00

1956
#591, Oriental Influence, 8", BKW
(Wendy Ann)
Mandarin coat lined to match dress,
Mandarin straw hat
$450.00 – 950.00

1956 – 1963
Groom, 8", BKW
(Wendy Ann)
Striped trousers and morning coat
$425.00 – 750.00

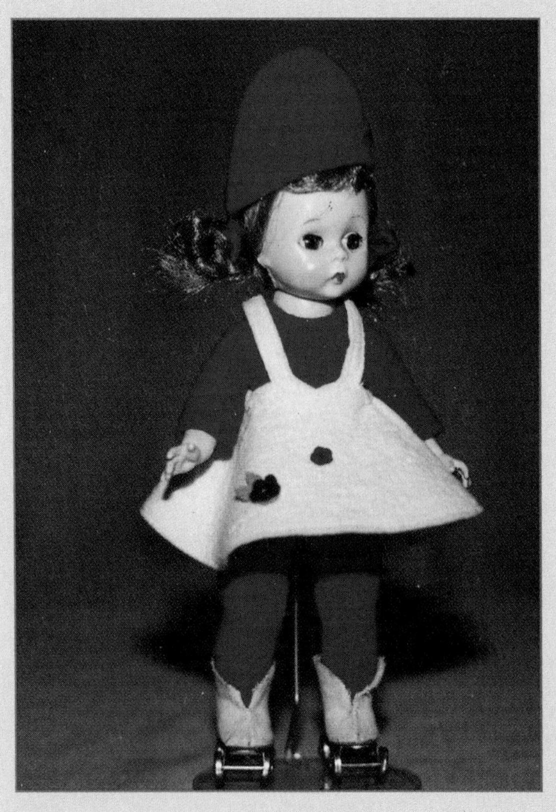

1956
#556, Wendy Roller Skating, 8", BKW
(Wendy Ann)
Felt skirt with red bodysuit and pixie cap
$550.00 – 950.00

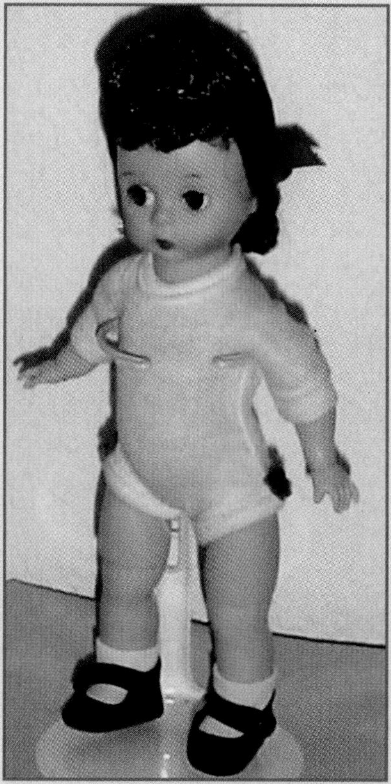

Wendy in a jersey bodysuit with felt flowers attached to each side with a metal brad
$325.00

1956
#553, Wendy Carries Her Milk Money
8", BKW
(Wendy Ann)
Cotton outfit, straw hat, and a purse for her milk money
$425.00 – 850.00

1956
Wendy, 8"
(Wendy Ann)
Organdy dress with taffeta pinafore
$450.00 – 850.00

1956
#539, A Very Special Hairdo, 8", BKW
(Wendy Ann)
Curl pulled to the back, outfit has special navy blue slip
Tag: "Alexander-kins"
$425.00 – 800.00

1956
#576, Sailor Dress, 8", BKW
(Wendy Ann)
Navy cotton dress with French sailor hat
$700.00 – 1,200.00

1956
#586, Wendy Goes Calling with Mother, 8", BKW
(Wendy Ann)
Organdy and lace dress with straw hat with lace
Tag: "Alexander-kins"
$375.00 – 800.00

1956
#561, Pierrot Clown, 8", BKW
Satin hat and suit with ruff of tulle, original dog
$575.00 – 1,000.00

1956
#588, Looks So Sweet, 8", BKW
(Wendy Ann)
Dotted nylon dress with straw hat
$450.00 – 900.00

1956
#594, Calls in a School Friend, 8", BKW
(Wendy Ann)
Striped organdy dress and straw hat
$425.00 – 850.00

1957
#432, Cousin Grace, 8", BKW
(Wendy Ann)
Mint and all original
$1,200.00 – 1,800.00

1957
#435, Aunt Pitty-Pat, 8", BKW
(Wendy Ann)
Checked dress with blue taffeta overdress, straw hat
$900.00 – 1,800.00

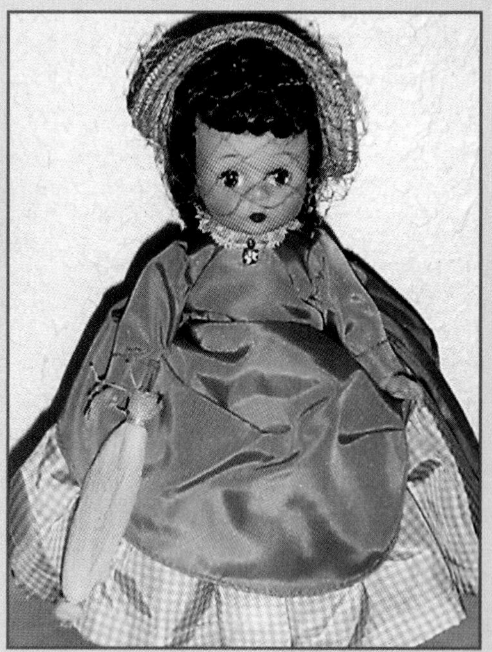

1957
#433, Nana the Governess, 8"
(Wendy)
$1,200.00 – 2,000.00

1957
#389, Wendy, 8"
(Wendy)
Velvet Party Dress
$1,200.00 – 2,000.00

1957
#434, Aunt Agatha, 8", BKW
(Wendy Ann)
Ante-bellum checked taffeta gown, black jacket, hat, and reticule
$1,200.00 – 2,000.00

1957
#344, Party Sundress, 8", BKW
(Wendy Ann)
Blue cotton dress and hat accented with gold
Tag: "Alexander-kins"
$550.00 – 900.00

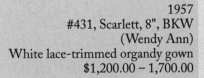

1957
#431, Scarlett, 8", BKW
(Wendy Ann)
White lace-trimmed organdy gown
$1,200.00 – 1,700.00

1957
#373, Rainy Day, 8", BKW
(Wendy Ann)
Vinyl coat and hat, came in various colors
$400.00 – 775.00.

1957
#395, First Communion, 8", BKW
(Wendy Ann)
Organdy dress with lace, tulle veil
$450.00 – 850.00

1957
#345, Wendy, 8", BKW
(Wendy Ann)
Polished cotton dress with Quaker collar
$450.00 – 900.00

1957
#376, First Long Party Dress, 8", BKW
(Wendy Ann)
Nylon dress has flower design instead of dotted
$750.00 – 1,200.00

1957
#338, Dressed for a Hot Morning, 8", BKW
(Wendy Ann)
Striped dress with button trim
$450.00 – 850.00

1957
#376, First Long Party Dress, 8", BKW
(Wendy Ann)
Green dotted nylon ribbon sash, trimmed in lace, bandeau with flowers on head
$750.00 – 1,200.00

1957
#371, Car Coat, 8", BKW
(Wendy Ann)
All original, hard to find doll
$900.00 – 1,800.00

1957
#376, First Long Party Dress
8", BKW
(Wendy Ann)
Pink dotted nylon with ribbon sash, pictured on cover of 1957 booklet, came in various colors
$750.00 – 1,200.00

1957
#380, Wendy Feels so Grown-Up, 8", BKW
(Wendy Ann)
Underneath the coat is a matching skirt and white blouse
$500.00 – 950.00

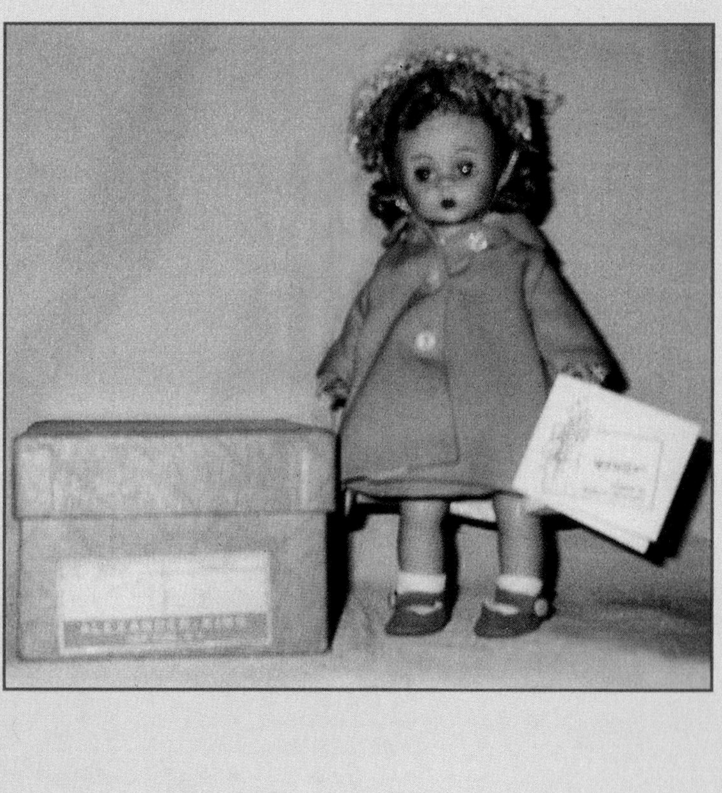

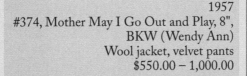

1957
#371, 8", Car Coat, BKW
(Wendy Ann)
Came in different colors, very rare doll
$900.00 – 1,800.00

1957
#374, Mother May I Go Out and Play, 8", BKW (Wendy Ann)
Wool jacket, velvet pants
$550.00 – 1,000.00

1957
#347, Bobby The Boy Next Door
8", BKW
(Wendy Ann)
$375.00 – 725.00

1957
#393, Wendy Dressed for Spectator Sports
8", BKW
(Wendy Ann)
$375.00 – 750.00

1957
#388E, Cherry Twin, 8", BKW
(Wendy Ann)
Organdy dress with embroidered cherries
$900.00 – 1,700.00

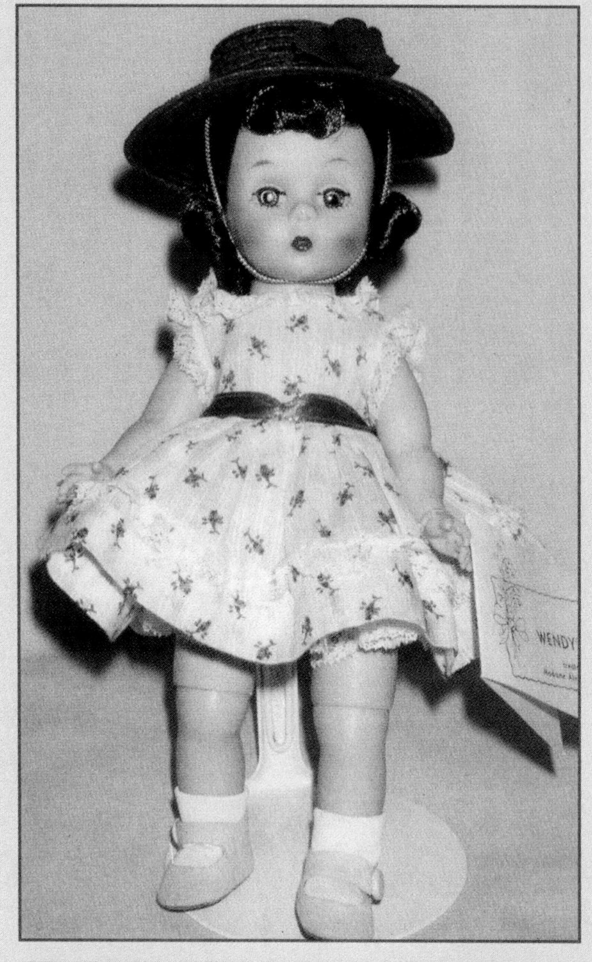

1957
#388, Wendy Dressed For a Party
8", BKW
(Wendy Ann)
Printed nylon dress, straw hat pictured different than one in catalog reprints
$375.00 – 800.00

1957
#386, Sweet Suggestion Wendy, 8", BKW
(Wendy Ann)
Sheer organdy of val lace, straw hat with flowers
$425.00 – 900.00

1957
#385, Wendy, 8", BKW
(Wendy Ann)
Striped cotton dress with lace bonnet
$400.00 – 800.00

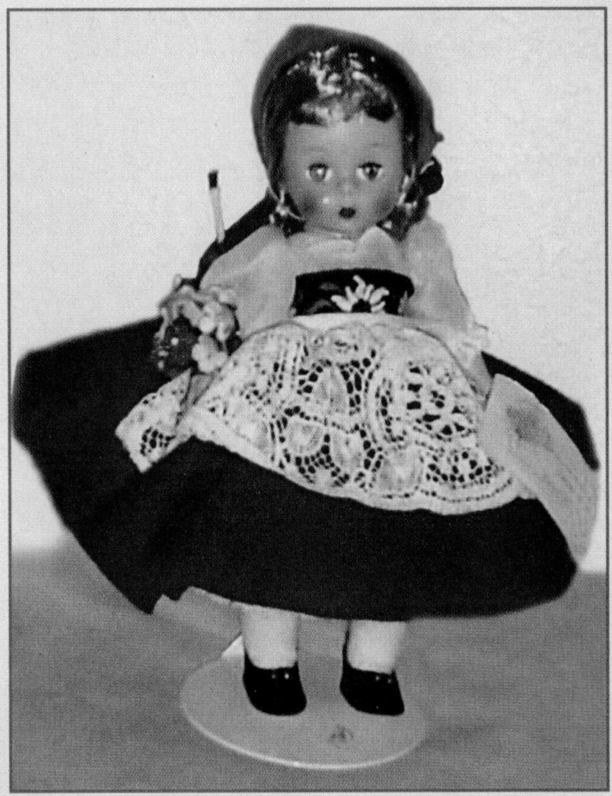

1957
#408, Wendy Bridesmaid, 8", BKW
(Wendy Ann)
Pink nylon dress, large picture hat
$900.00 – 1,600.00

1957
#411, Little Minister
Extremely rare
Shown with Quiz-kin
Bride and Groom
from 1953
Little Minister, $3,000.00+
Bride, $500.00 – 900.00
Groom, $400.00 – 800.00

1958
#540, Wendy Learning to Skate, 8", BKW
(Wendy Ann)
Felt skirt with tulle
Tag: "Alexander-kin"
$425.00 – 850.00

1958
#575, Wendy Going to Grandmother's House
8", BKW
(Wendy Ann)
Striped cotton dress, pictured with different hat than is in reprints
$375.00 – 750.00

1958
Wendy, 8", BKW
(Wendy Ann)
Blue nylon dress with flocked dots, uncataloged doll
$400.00 – 850.00

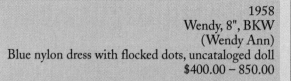

1958
#524, Wendy's Rain Set
8", BKW
(Wendy Ann)
Reversible raincoat
and hat
Tag: "Alexander-kin"
$425.00 – 800.00

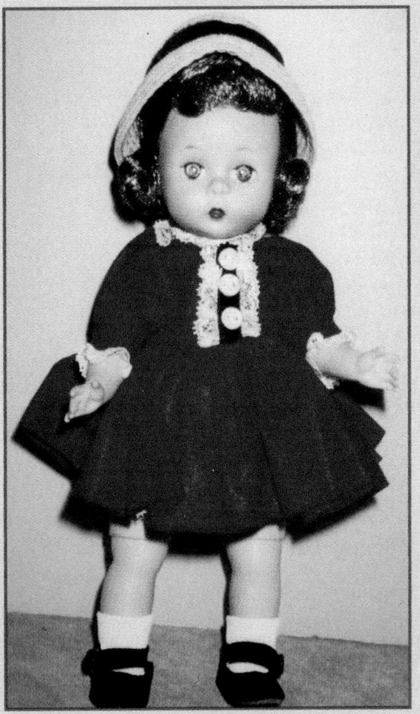

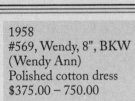

1958
#569, Wendy, 8", BKW
(Wendy Ann)
Polished cotton dress
$375.00 – 750.00

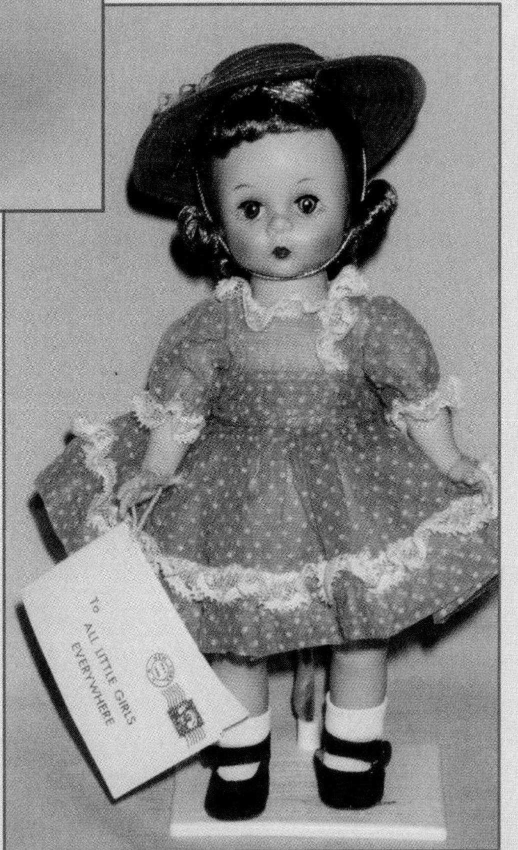

1958
#566, "Wendy Adores a Party," 8", BKW
(Wendy Ann)
Dotted nylon dress trimmed with lace
$425.00 – 850.00

1958
#568, "Wendy Goes to the Carousel," 8", BKW
(Wendy Ann)
Cotton dress, hard to find doll
$425.00 – 900.00

1958
#530, Wendy Looks Cool and Summery, 8", BKW
(Wendy Ann)
Cotton print dress and hat trimmed in lace
$400.00 – 825.00

1958
#546, Wendy's Morning Dress, 8", BKW
(Wendy Ann)
Cotton dress
$375.00 – 750.00

1958
#565, "Wendy in an Organdy Party Dress," 8", BKW
(Wendy Ann)
Organdy dress trimmed in lace
$450.00 – 900.00

1958
#561, Wendy Goes to the Circus, 8", BKW
(Wendy Ann)
Cotton dress and pinafore, straw hat
$425.00 – 850.00

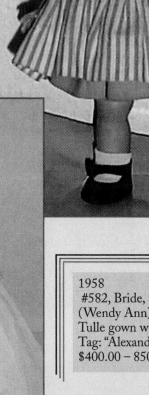

1958
#582, Bride, 8", BKW
(Wendy Ann)
Tulle gown with lace bodice
Tag: "Alexander-kin"
$400.00 – 850.00

1959
#483, Wendy Pink Bride, 8", BKW
(Wendy Ann)
Very rare bride in pink tulle
$900.00 – 1,500.00

1959
Wendy, 8", BKW
(Wendy Ann)
Boxed outfit, uncataloged, thought to be 1959
Boxed outfit, $150.00

1959
Ballerina, 8", BKW
(Wendy Ann)
Gold cloth top trimmed in
sequins with gold net tutu,
sequin tara
$550.00 – 1,000.00

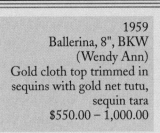

1959
#433, Wendy, 8", BKW
(Wendy Ann)
Plain and striped cotton combination dress, different white straw hat than is pictured in catalog reprints
$375.00 – 800.00

1959
Wendy, 8", BKW
(Wendy Ann)
Polished cotton dress and pinafore, a rare doll
$650.00 – 1,100.00

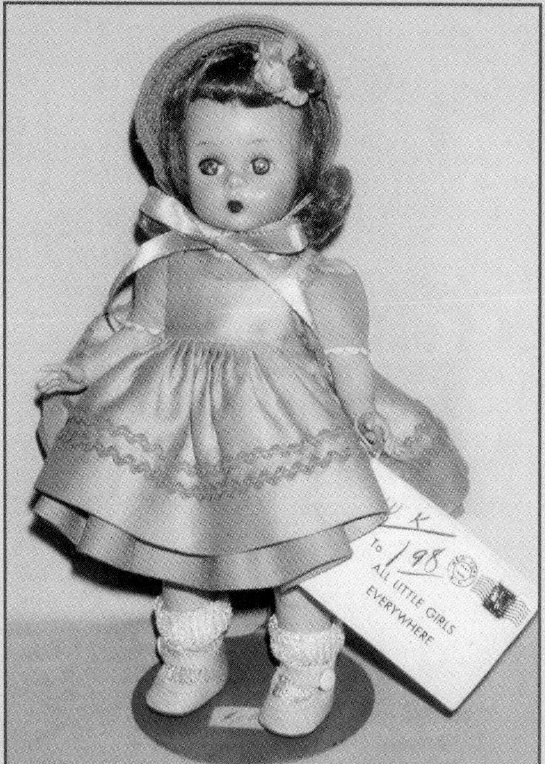

1959
#444, Wendy's Favorite Summer Afternoon Outfit, 8", BKW
(Wendy Ann)
Organdy dress with dotted swiss pinafore
Tag: "Alexander-kins"
$450.00 – 850.00

1960
#598, Maggie Mixup, 8", BKW
(Maggie)
Checked cotton dress with pinafore, straw hat with rosebud, green eyes, and red long straight hair
$425.00 – 800.00

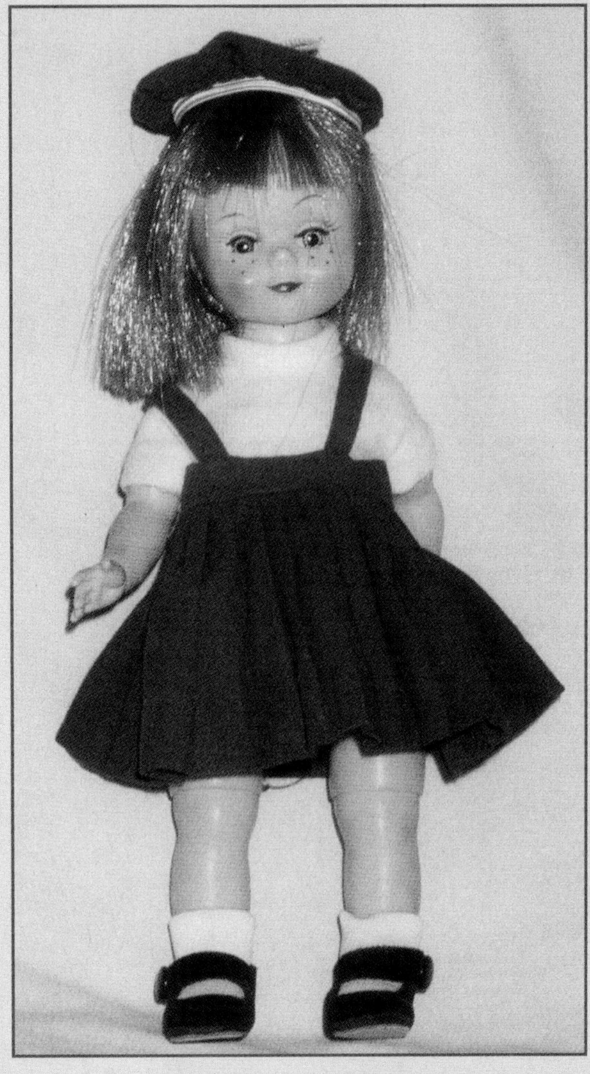

1960
#597, Maggie Mixup, 8", BKW
(Maggie)
Pleated skirt, jersey sweater, and sailor hat
$400.00 – 750.00

1960
#593, Wendy Loves to Roller Skate, 8", BKW
(Maggie)
Plaid skirt, pique shirt, and felt hat, brown roller skates
$550.00 – 850.00

1960
#1050, Little Lady Set, 8", BKW
(Maggie)
Cotton dress and pinafore, shadow box for framing, plus toileties of bubble bath, toilet water, and perfume
$1,200.00

1960
#340, Wendy in a Cute Outfit, 8", BKW
(Wendy Ann)
Polished cotton dress with organdy yoke and sleeves
$425.00 – 850.00

1960
#327, Wendy Dressed for Shopping, 8", BKW
(Wendy Ann)
Cotton dress
Tag: "Alexander-kins"
$425.00 – 800.00

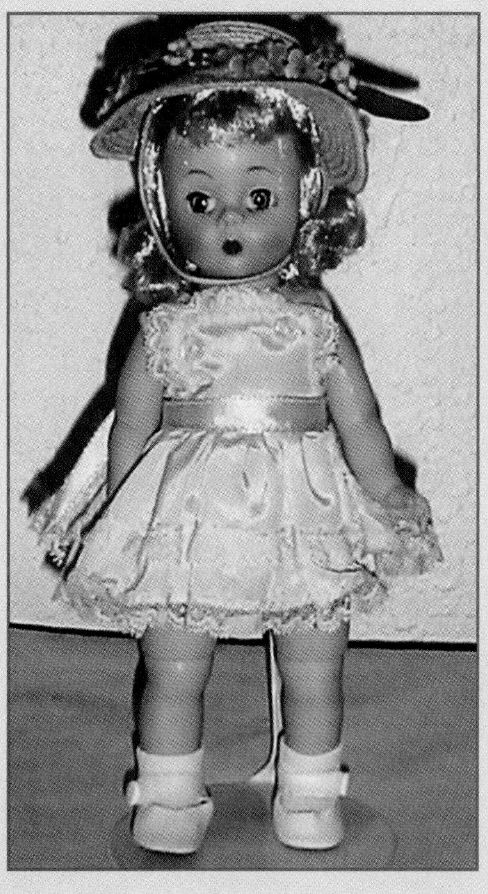

Wendy, 8", BKW
(Wendy Ann)
Taffeta dress trimmed in lace, straw hat
$375.00 – 800.00

Wendy, 8", BKW
(Wendy Ann)
Cotton print dress, straw hat
$350.00 – 750.00

Wendy, 8", BKW
(Wendy Ann)
Print cotton dress, straw hat
$375.00 – 775.00

1960 – 1961
Maggie Mixup, 8", BKW
(Maggie)
Striped cotton pants
with red felt flowers,
cotton shirt
Tag: "Maggie"
$425.00 – 850.00

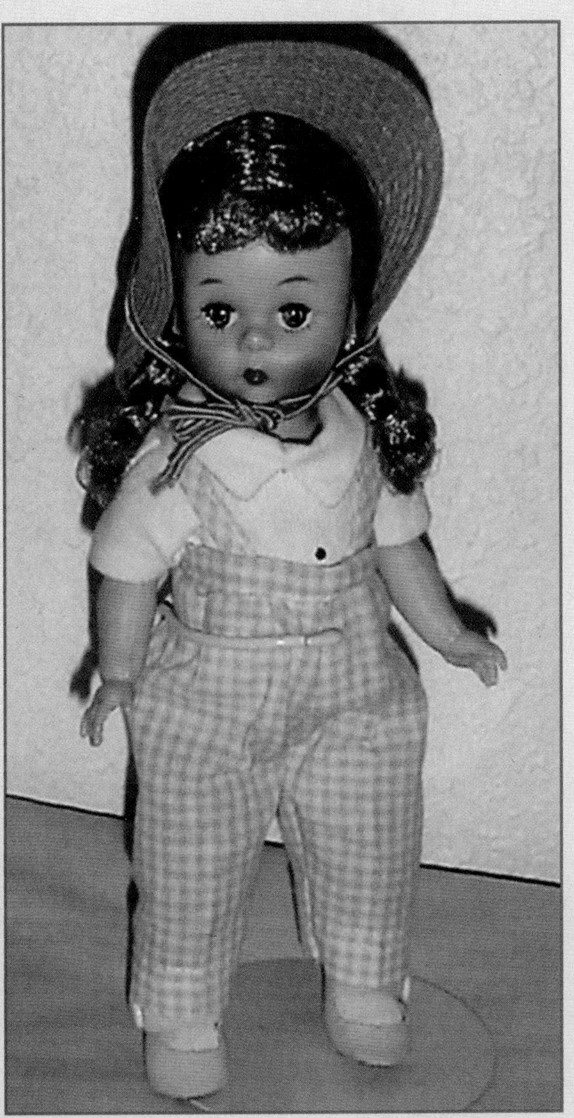

Early 1960s
Wendy, 8", BKW
(Wendy Ann)
Pique top with checked pants, straw hat
$450.00 – 900.00

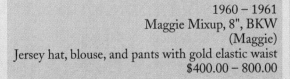

1960 – 1961
Maggie Mixup, 8", BKW
(Maggie)
Jersey hat, blouse, and pants with gold elastic waist
$400.00 – 800.00

1960 – 1961
Maggie Mixup, 8", BKW
(Wendy)
FAO Schwarz exclusive
Freckles and red straight hair, felt jumper, jersey top
$500.00 – 1,000.00

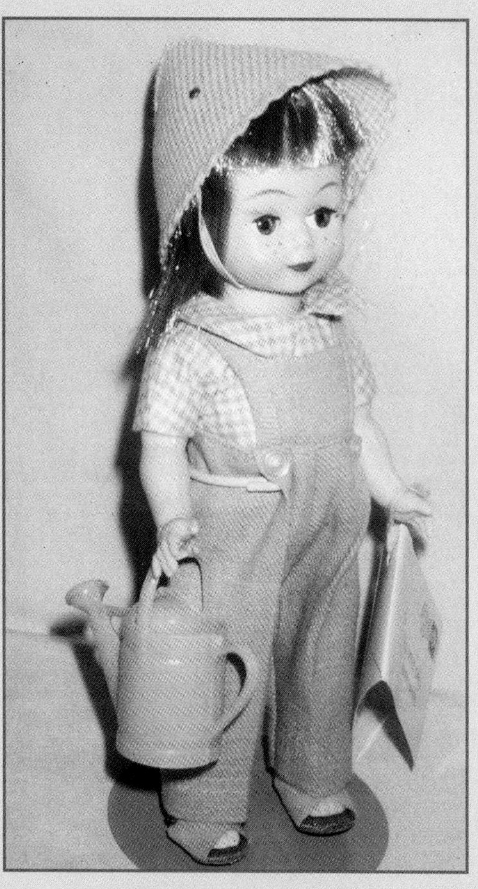

1961
#610, Maggie Mixup, 8", BKW
(Maggie)
Overalls, checked cotton shirt, and sun hat, original watering can
$550.00 – 1,000.00

1961
#617, Maggie Mixup, 8", BKW
(Maggie)
Check cotton dress with sash, straw hat with ribbons
$375.00 – 800.00

1961
#627, Maggie Mixup, 8", BKW
(Maggie)
Frilly cotton dress with lace, straw hat,
original dog Danger
$550.00 – 1,000.00

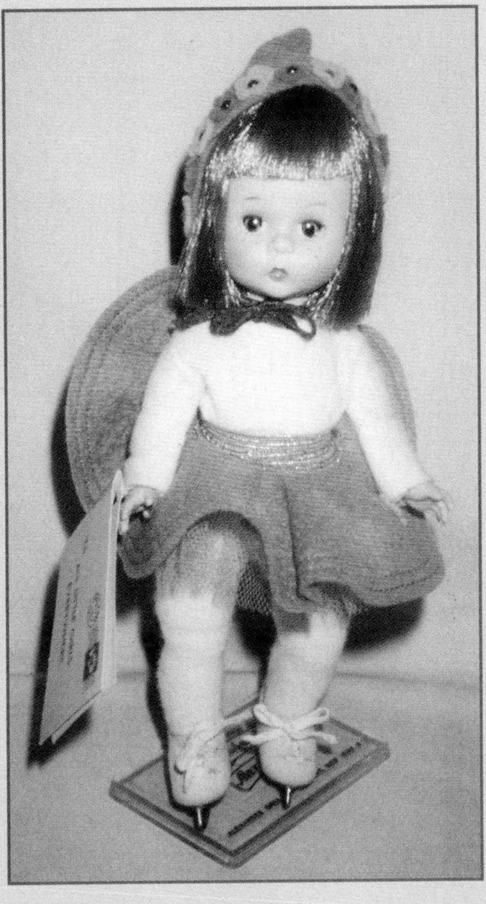

1961
#626, Maggie Mixup, 8", BKW
(Wendy Ann with freckles)
Felt skirt, hat, and jersey bodysuit, white ice skates
$550.00 – 950.00

1961
#618, Maggie Mixup Angel, 8", BKW
(Maggie)
Lighter shade of blue taffeta
$550.00 – 900.00

1961
#0618, Maggie Mixup Angel
Mint in original box, taffeta outfit with silver wings
$450.00

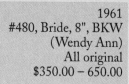

1961
#480, Bride, 8", BKW
(Wendy Ann)
All original
$350.00 – 650.00

1961
#485, Charity, 8", BKW
(Wendy)
Americana Group
Blue cotton dress, organdy blouse, and straw hat
$2,000.00+

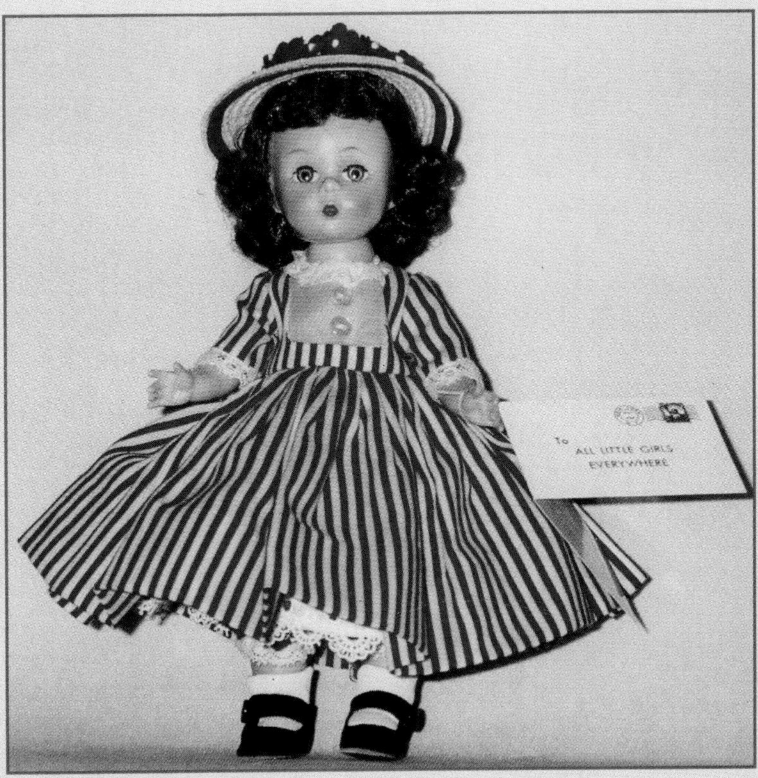

1961
#488, "Lucy," 8", BKW
(Wendy Ann)
Americana Group
Striped cotton dress with organdy yoke
$2,100.00+

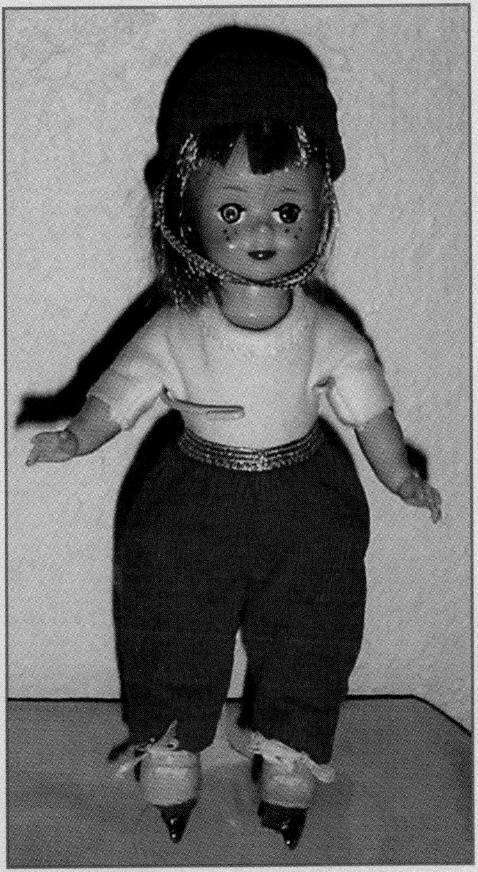

1960 – 1961
Maggie Mixup, 8", BKW
(Maggie)
Jersey sweater, velvet pants and cap, boxed outfit
$525.00 – 850.00

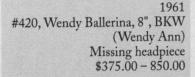

1961
#420, Wendy Ballerina, 8", BKW
(Wendy Ann)
Missing headpiece
$375.00 – 850.00

1961
#420, Wendy Ballerina, 8", BKW
(Wendy Ann)
Rare yellow costume
$500.00 – 950.00

1962
#352, Wendy Dressed for a Summer Day, 8", BKW
(Wendy Ann)
Print cotton dress and straw hat with flowers
Tag: "Wendy-kin"
$400.00 – 800.00

1962
#640, Wendy Ballerina, 8", BKW
(Wendy Ann)
Pink, satin, and tulle ballet outfit
Tag: Madame Alexander, etc.
$325.00 – 650.00

1963
#465, Cousin Marie, 8", BKW
(Wendy Ann)
Cotton dress with pinafore
$425.00 – 900.00

1965
#383, Bo Peep, 8", BKW
(Wendy Ann)
Plastic lamb attached to wrist
Tag: Madame Alexander, etc.
$275.00 – 525.00

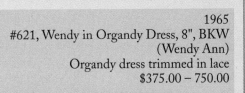

1965
#621, Wendy in Organdy Dress, 8", BKW
(Wendy Ann)
Organdy dress trimmed in lace
$375.00 – 750.00

1965
#622, Wendy, 8", BKW
(Wendy Ann)
Cotton dress with hair pulled up to crown
and braided in back
$425.00 – 750.00

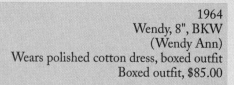

1964
Wendy, 8", BKW
(Wendy Ann)
Wears polished cotton dress, boxed outfit
Boxed outfit, $85.00

1964
#0464, Wendy, 8", BKW
(Wendy Ann)
Boxed outfit of cotton dress and felt jacket
Boxed outfit, $95.00

1965
McGuffey Ana, 8", BKW
(Wendy Ann)
Checked cotton dress with organdy pinafore
$350.00 – 700.00

1963 – 1964, #760
1965, #630
Wendy Bride, 8", BKW
(Wendy Ann)
Organdy dress with tiers of lace
$325.00 – 650.00

1965
#785, Scarlett, 8", BKW
(Wendy Ann)
White taffeta dress with rosebuds at hem, straw hat with roses
Tag: "Scarlett"
$600.00 – 950.00

1962 – 1965
Tyrolean Girl, 8", BKW
(Wendy Ann)
Velvet top, cotton skirt, eyelet pinafore, felt hat
$125.00 – 250.00

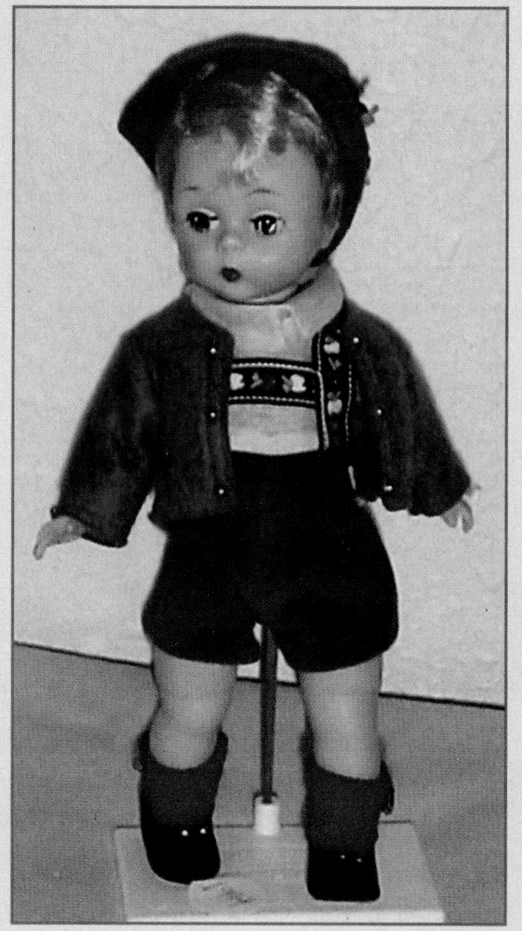

1962 – 1965
Tyrolean Boy, 8", BKW
(Wendy Ann)
Velvet pants attached to cotton top, felt jacket and hat
$125.00 – 250.00

1961 – 1965
Swiss, 8", BKW
(Wendy Ann)
Felt skirt attached to organdy top, felt hat and lace apron
$125.00 – 250.00

1965
#772, Argentine Boy, 8", BKW
(Wendy Ann)
Black felt jacket and hat, cotton pants
attached to a white top
$200.00 – 450.00

1965
Spanish Boy,
8",
BKW
(Wendy Ann)
$150.00 – 350.00

1965 – 1968
Greek Boy, 8", BKW
White dress, felt jacket
and hat
$150.00 – 375.00

Argentine Boy,
8", BKW
$200.00 – 450.00

Peruvian Boy,
8", BKW
Cotton serape tweed
pants, felt hat
$175.00 – 450.00

1961
Spanish Girl, 8", BKW
(Wendy Ann)
Red cotton dress with tiers trimmed in lace, lace mantilla
$125.00 – 250.00

1965
Spanish Boy, 8", BKW
(Wendy Ann)
Cotton pants, felt jacket and hat
$150.00 – 350.00

1965
#771, Argentine Girl, 8", BKW
(Wendy Ann)
Cotton dress and apron, taffeta scarf
$125.00 – 250.00

Babies

Madame Alexander has made baby dolls all through the years. Mothers often purchased baby dolls for their children to play with while placing more elaborate expensive dolls on display. Baby dolls have been primarily play dolls and have not increased in value as other dolls that were made the same year. There are exceptions such as Little Genius and Littlest Kitten.

1954
#3565, Christening Baby, 13"
Vinyl doll, organdy dress trimmed in lace
$100.00 – 250.00

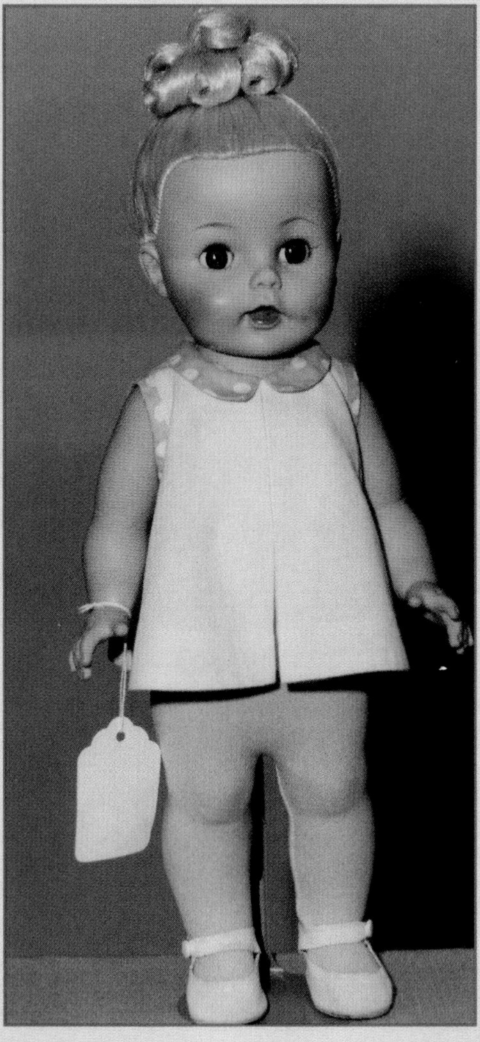

1961
Mary Sunshine, 15"
Only fully jointed plastic/vinyl doll, original clothes
$175.00 – 350.00

1963
#2930, Little Shaver, 12"
Plastic/vinyl
$125.00 – 250.00

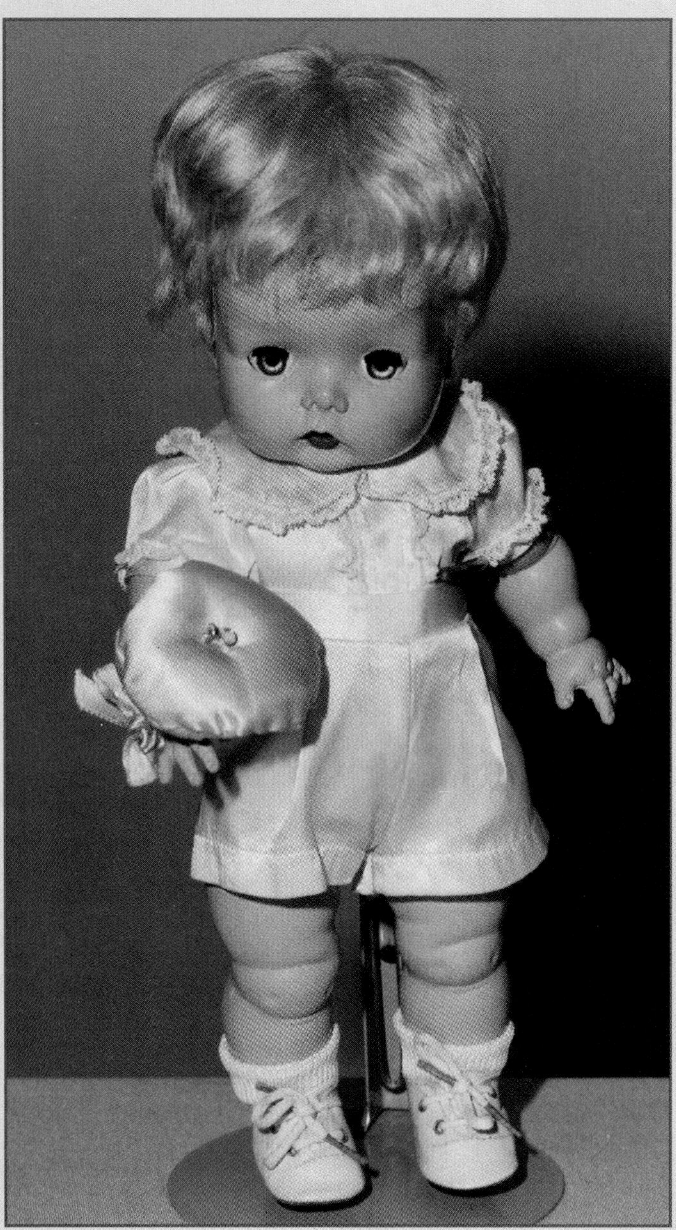

1951
Precious, 12"
Ringbearer outfit of satin and lace, hard plastic, all original
$400.00 – 850.00

1948 – 1951
Precious, 12"
All hard plastic, original yellow tagged dress
$150.00 – 350.00

1959
Kathleen Toddler, 23"
Rigid vinyl, original clothes
$125.00 – 300.00

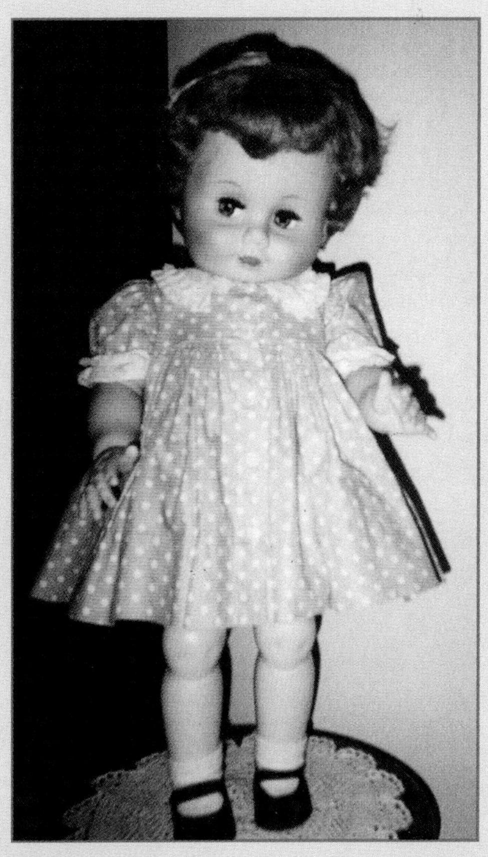

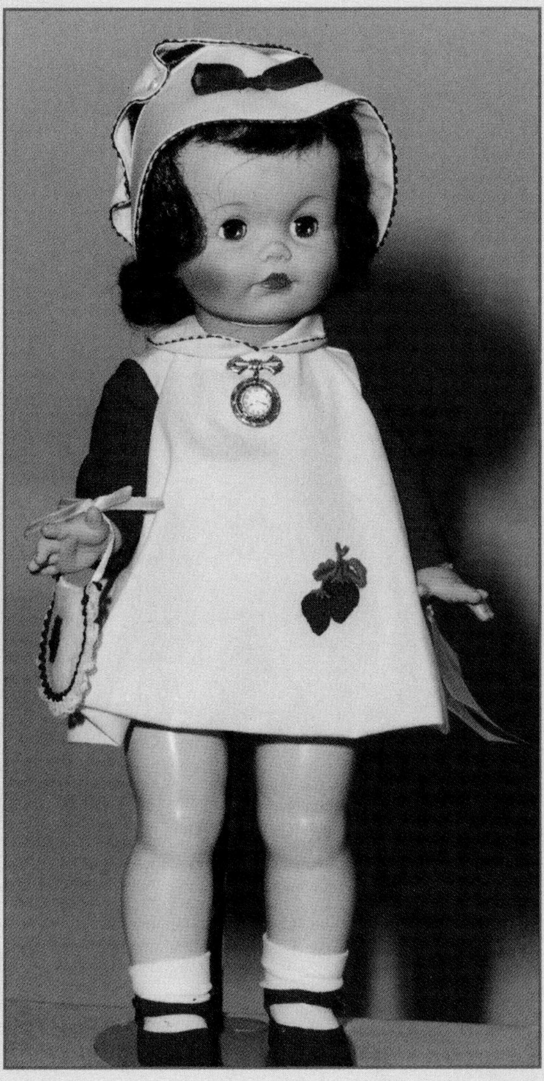

1964
#1830, Binnie, 18"
Plastic/vinyl, all original
$175.00 – 500.00

1964
#1820, Binnie, 18"
Replaced shoes
$175.00 – 475.00

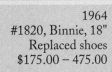

Brenda Starr

Brenda Starr was a beautiful newspaper reporter in a comic strip. She was manufactured by Madame Alexander in 1964 only. Brenda Starr was 12" tall, had red rooted hair, blue sleep eyes, and pierced ears. The body had vinyl arms and head, legs jointed at the knees, a high heel feet, and a rigid plastic body. She came dressed as well as in window box sets with hairpieces, curlers, comb, etc. Boxed outfits were also sold separately. Among the wardrobe available were dresses, evening gowns, beach wear, rain coat sets, and lingerie. Dolls were also sold as basic dolls wearing a chemise.

In 1965 the Brenda Starr doll became Yolanda. Instead of having red hair, Yolanda has blond hair and green eyes. Yolanda is shown in the 1965 catalog as being available in a turquoise satin formal with sequin trim, as a bride in a ruffled lace gown, and in a pink bouffant pleated tulle gown.

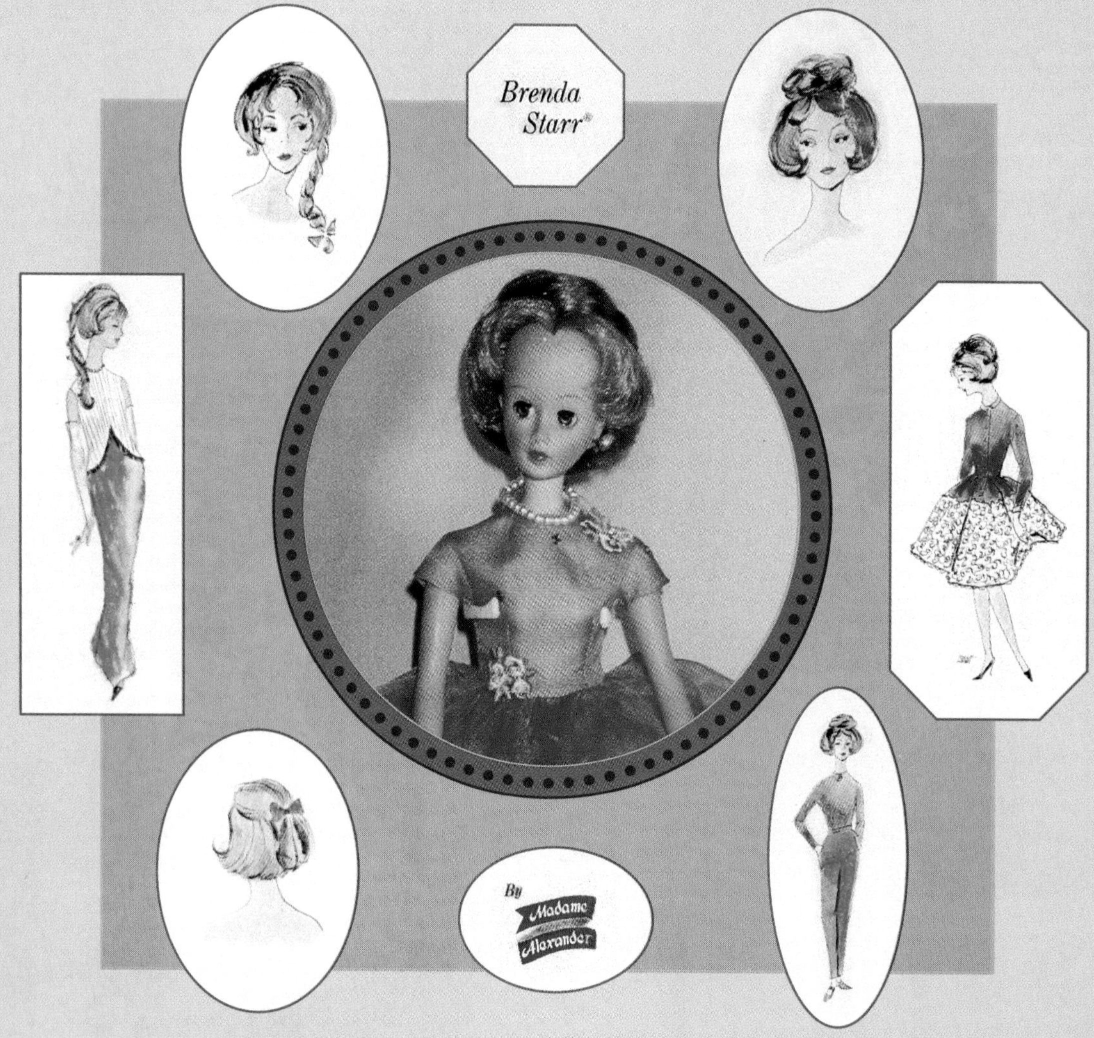

1964
#900, Brenda Starr, 12"
In basic chemise, mint in original box
$125.00 – 275.00

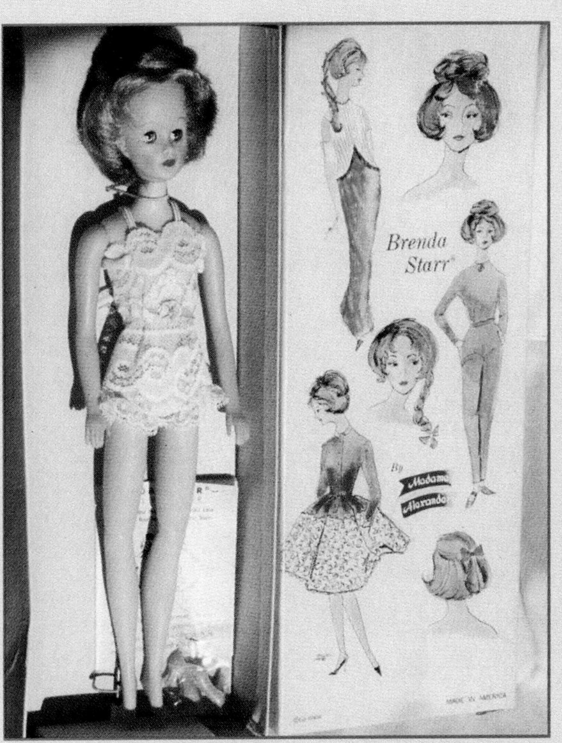

1964
Brenda Starr, 12"
In original organdy ballgown
$225.00 – 475.00

1964
Brenda Starr, 12"
Silver evening gown
$150.00 – 400.00

1964
#920, Brenda Starr, 12"
Dressed for a ball at the Press Club
Mint in box
$175.00 – 475.00

1964
#900, Brenda Starr, 12"
Basic dolls, clothes were sold separately
$125.00 – 275.00, each

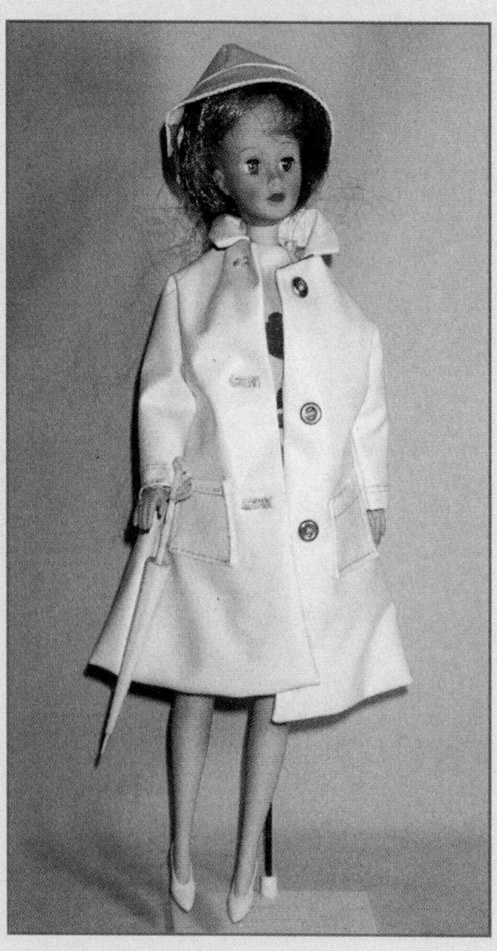

1964
Brenda Starr, 12"
All original, in her rainy day outfit
$150.00 – 325.00

1964
#921, Brenda Starr, 12"
Combination dress and cape fastened at shoulder with tiny roses
$175.00 – 400.00

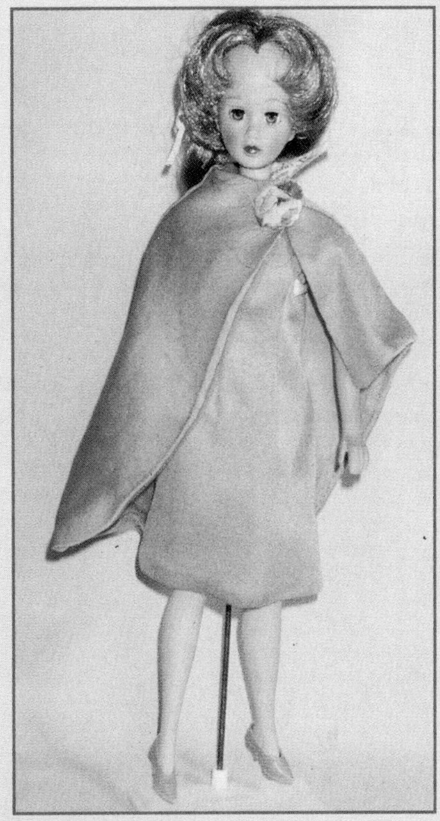

1965
#1030, Yolanda Bride, 12"
(Brenda Starr)
Missing bouquet, but all original otherwise
$225.00 – 450.00

1964
#975, Brenda Starr, 12"
Sheath dress with extra wig, comb
$175.00 – 475.00

Cissette is a hard plastic doll that is 10" to 11" tall and was made from 1957 to 1963. She has an adult type body with jointed knees and high heel feet. The 1959 Sleeping Beauty was made with the Cissette face and body but with flat feet. On the back most of the dolls have "MME/Alexander." Her clothing was tagged "Cissette." She came as a dressed doll or as a basic doll in a chemise with dozens of extra boxed outfits that could be purchased separately. Many were never listed in the catalog. This doll was reintroduced in 1987 and is in the Alexander doll line today.

The Jacqueline dolls were made with the Cissette face and body in 1961 and 1962. She had polished nails, blue eyelids, eyeliner, and a dark wig with a curl on the forehead. Margot was made in 1961 with the same style except she had elaborate upswept hairdos.

1963, #765, Cissette Queen

1957
Cissette
Shoes and hose sold separately
Pictured are the hard to find green elastic high heels.
Shoes, $75.00
Hose, $35.00

1957
#971, Cissette as Queen Elizabeth II
Gown of gold brocade, worn with the blue sash of the garter, golden coronet
$350.00 – 700.00

1957
#974, 10"
Cissette dressed for the theatre
Sheath gown with a flounce of dotted nylon tulle, jeweled bracelet and earrings, pearl necklace
$700.00 – 1,200.00

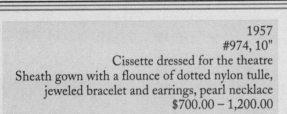

1957
#975, Cissette as Lady Hamilton
Pink silk gown, large picture hat
$650.00 – 1,200.00

1957
#912, Cissette in a navy taffeta jumper type dress with pink silk sleeves and bodice
Wrong hat and shoes for this outfit
$325.00 – 775.00

1957
#0927, Cissette in a boxed outfit, coat and hat lined in pink
Boxed outfit, $200.00

1957
#973
Cissette in the rare green velvet gown and orlon stole, also came in black velvet
$700.00 – 1,100.00

1957
#0925
Cissette in a boxed coat and hat set
Boxed outfit, $200.00

1957
#976, 10"
Cissette wearing a short satin theatre dress with matching coat
$475.00 – 900.00

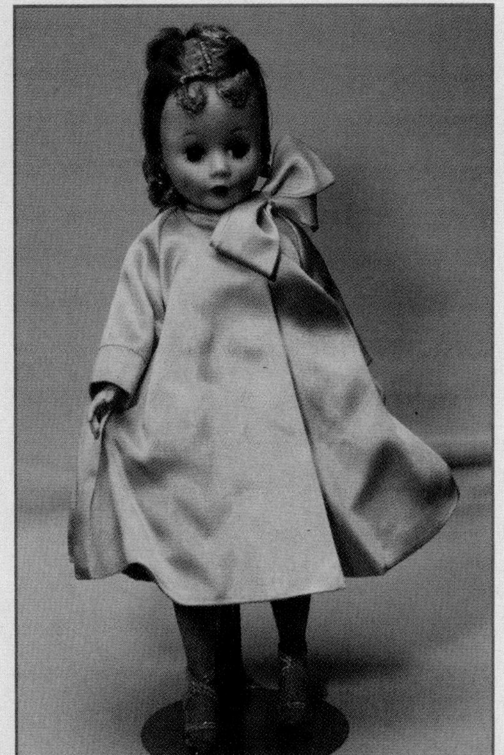

1957
#943
Cissette is going to a matinee
Lilac taffeta dress and jacket, straw hat with flowers
Missing purse
$275.00 – 700.00

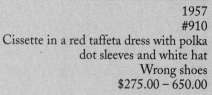

1957
#910
Cissette in a red taffeta dress with polka dot sleeves and white hat
Wrong shoes
$275.00 – 650.00

1957
#918
Cissette is ready for tea with a friend in this taffeta dress and straw hat
$325.00 – 750.00

1957
#930
Cissette in a blue shirtwaist dress of polished cotton with val lace trim, straw hat with roses
$300.00 – 775.00

1957
#0924, 10"
Cissette wearing a wool felt skirt, silk shirt, sold as outfit only, dog added
Boxed outfit, $175.00

1957
#0925
Cissette wearing felt coat with matching hat, sold as outfit only
Boxed outfit, $200.00

1957
#916, 10"
Cissette dressed in a taffeta dress with sleeves and bodice inset of dotted organdy, white straw cloche hat
$325.00 – 750.00

1957
Cissette (left) and Wendy (right) wearing matching print gowns and robes
Boxed outfits, $75.00 each

1957
#0931
Cissette in a boxed outfit, can be reversed to navy
Boxed outfit, $150.00

1957
#909, 10"
Cissette in summer cotton dress and straw hat with flowers
$275.00 – 675.00

1958
#839, 10"
Cissette in a cotton jumper dress with pink blouse and straw hat
$300.00 – 700.00

1958
Extra boxed outfit for Cissette
Also came as a boxed doll
$325.00 – 800.00

1958
#838, 10"
Cissette is a vision in pink with rhinestones and perfect little flowers
$325.00 – 850.00

1958
#873
Cissette in bridal gown with wreath pattern skirt that matches Cissy and Elise
$400.00 – 900.00

1958
Cissette in a rare variation of the 1958 yellow outfit with lace
Tag: "Cissette"
$375.00 – 975.00

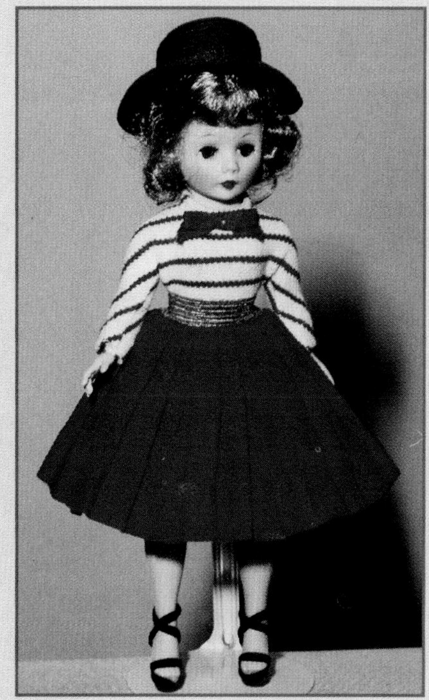

1958
#832
Cissette dressed for a seagoing adventure, red pleated skirt, and straw hat
Issued with rare "coin" earrings
Also shown with jacket
$450.00 – 875.00

1958
Cissette in an uncataloged boxed outfit, skirt came in different prints
Boxed outfit, $200.00

1958
10"
Cissette in a boxed outfit that could be purchased separately
Boxed outfit, $150.00

1958
#825
Cissette twins in velvet pants attached to a gold elastic waist, white nylon blouse
$300.00 – 700.00 each

1958
#815, 10"
Cissette in a print cotton skirt and jersey blouse
$325.00 – 775.00

1958
Cissette in a tagged but uncataloged outfit
$450.00

1958
#836
FAO Schwarz store special
Yellow dotted swiss
$500.00 – 950.00

1958
FAO Schwarz store special
Very rare, navy taffeta cape
$450.00 – 950.00

1958
Cissette in a FAO Schwarz store special variation of similar style; this dress is turquoise, much fancier pink hat
MIB
$550.00 – 900.00

1958
Cissette in a tagged FAO Schwarz special, very frilly party dress
$475.00 – 850.00

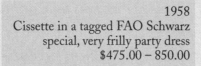

1958
Cissette in a tagged uncataloged outfit
$400.00 – 750.00

Very rare twin Cissettes made in USA, FAO Schwarz special, labeled on boxes
$400.00 – 850.00

Cissette houndstooth coat with matching tagged pleated skirt and black knit top, same coat made for Wendy and Lissy
$450.00 – 800.00

1958
#852, 10"
Cissette Bridesmaid, tulle gown decorated with flowers and rhinestones, picture hat
$450.00 – 900.00

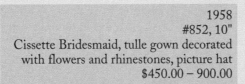

1958
#0895
Cissette dressed in a boxed outfit
Heavy slipper satin dress
Boxed outfit, $250.00

1958
Cissette in an uncataloged boxed outfit, glasses added
Boxed outfit, $200.00

1958
Cissette in a boxed outfit, extremely rare
Blue velvet dress and jacket
Fabulous hat
$900.00 – 1,600.00

1959
10"
Cissette in a very elaborate gold ballgown
$350.00 – 800.00

1959
#731, 10"
Cissette in an exquisite lace dress with tulle and flower hat
$600.00 – 1,200.00

1959
#741
Cissette dressed as a bridesmaid in pleated nylon dress and a large picture hat
$375.00 – 850.00

1959
Cissette in a boxed fuchsia coat and hat outfit also made for Elise
Boxed outfit, $250.00

1959
#742, Cissette as Queen
White brocade gown trimmed in jewels
$350.00 – 650.00

1959
Sleeping Beauty with Cissette face
Taffeta gown trimmed in gold, only Cissette made with flat feet, made exclusively for Disney
$275.00 – 600.00

1959
Cissette in a labeled but uncataloged outfit, the cape is faille taffeta on the outside with the lining matching the dress
$700.00 – 1,400.00

1959
Cissette's dress has bodice darts, untrimmed white cloche hat
Red dress with dots
$325.00 – 700.00

1959
Cissette in an uncataloged tagged outfit
$375.00 – 700.00

1960
#842, Cissette Queen
Brocade gown, gold elastic bracelet with jewels
$400.00 – 750.00

1960
#813, 10"
Cissette in an original outfit, vinyl pointed ballet shoes
$325.00 – 750.00

Probably 1960
No bodice darts, which reflects Cissette clothing dating from 1960 to 1963
$350.00 – 750.00

1960
#810
Cissette in a polished cotton dress and lace-trimmed organdy
$375.00 – 850.00

1960
Cissette in a tagged outfit
White top, gloves pinned to skirt
$325.00 – 750.00

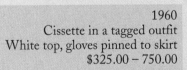

1961
#824
Cissette in a long formal gown of gold cloth with a gold net stole, rhinestone earrings
$350.00 – 775.00

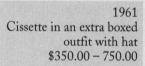

1961
Cissette in an extra boxed outfit with hat
$350.00 – 750.00

1961
#0846
Cissette in a boxed outfit that came in a variation of prints
$350.00 – 750.00

1961
#920 Margot with Cissette face
Purple satin gown with sequin straps,
triple drop rhinestone earrings
$400.00 – 900.00

1961
#920
Margot with Cissette face
Lavender satin, this variation has matching stole
$375.00 – 850.00

1961
#806
Cissette in a cotton one-piece sunsuit
with removable skirt
Basket added, should have
red plastic case
$300.00 – 650.00

1961
#811
Cissette in a polished cotton dress, straw hat
$350.00 – 700.00

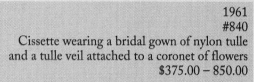

1961
#840
Cissette wearing a bridal gown of nylon tulle and a tulle veil attached to a coronet of flowers
$375.00 – 850.00

1961
10"
Cissette in a tagged, very hard to find outfit
$350.00 – 750.00

1961
#0970
Margot with Cissette face
Coat of pink pique and matching hat
Replaced shoes
Boxed outfit, $175.00

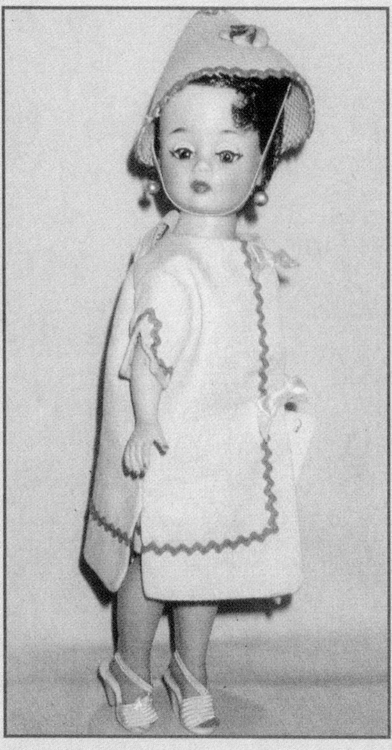

1961
Margot with Cissette face
Boxed tagged outfit
Orange pants, striped top
Boxed outfit, $300.00

1961
Margot with Cissette face
Tagged boxed pegnoir set
Boxed set, $225.00

1962
#763, Cissette Queen
Brocade gown with jewels on skirt
$425.00 – 750.00

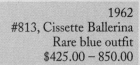

1962
#813, Cissette Ballerina
Rare blue outfit
$425.00 – 850.00

1962
Cissette in a tagged cotton dress with eyelet trim at the hem, blue striped version of square dance dress
$400.00 – 775.00

1962
10"
Cissette in a boxed outfit
Boxed outfit, $95.00

1962
Cissette in boxed outfit, felt jacket and hat
Boxed outfit, $125.00

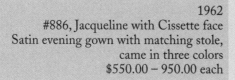

1962
#886, Jacqueline with Cissette face
Satin evening gown with matching stole,
came in three colors
$550.00 – 950.00 each

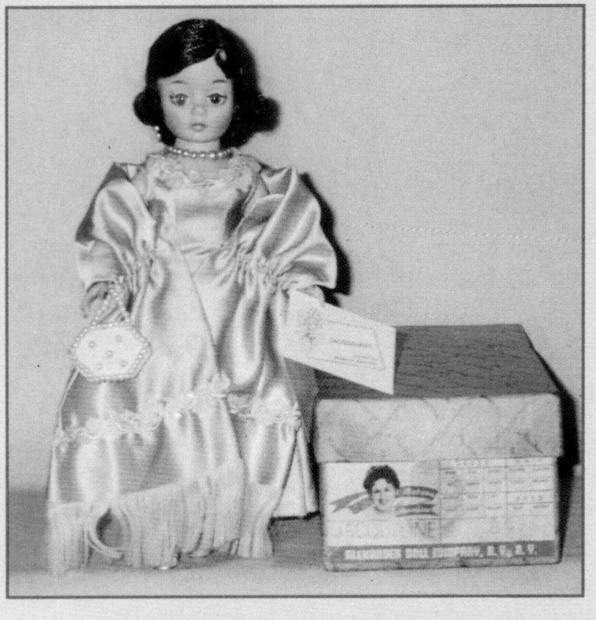

1962
#886, Jacqueline with Cissette face
Satin evening gown with matching stole, came in three colors
$950.00

1962
10", Jacqueline with Cissette face
Blue cotton pants, jersey blouse, and leather type jacket, dog added
$600.00 – 900.00

1963
#0732
Cissette in a separate boxed outfit
Boxed outfit, $300.00

1963
#765, Bubblecut Queen
Rare, MIB
Blue rhinestone ring and double drop rhinestone earrings
Probably made with left over bubble cut dolls
Same dress as more common 1963 Queen
$400.00 – 850.00

1963
#765, Cissette as Queen
Brocade gown with the sash of the garter
$375.00 – 700.00

1963
#740, 10"
Cissette in a satin ballgown, also came in blue
$550.00 – 950.00

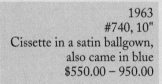

1963
#755
Cissette in a tulle gown with three rows of lace at the hem, veil attached to a coronet of flowers
$400.00 – 850.00

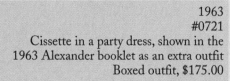

1963
#0721
Cissette in a party dress, shown in the 1963 Alexander booklet as an extra outfit
Boxed outfit, $175.00

1963
Cissette as Gold Rush
Orange long dress with bustle and straw hat with net, feathers and orange ribbon
$700.00 – 1,400.00

1963
#745
Cissette in a lace ruffled gown, also came in pink and blue
$375.00 – 850.00

Cissy

The Cissy face was first used on the Winnie doll in 1953. Winnie was a walking doll made of hard plastic with a little girl's body with flat feet. She was made in 15", 18", and 25" sizes. She had sleep eyes and a glued-on wig. In 1955 Cissy was made with an adult body with the Winnie head in the 20" to 21" size. Cissy was made from 1955 to 1962. In 1990 the Alexander Company made Me and My Scassi with the vinyl Cissy head. In 1996 Cissy was reintroduced as part of the Alexander line and continues today. The popularity of the Cissy doll has insured that this face will forever be known as Cissy. The body and legs with high heel feet were made of hard plastic while the oversleeved arms are made of vinyl and are jointed at the elbow. (Oversleeved arm is a term used by Cissy collectors for the two-piece vinyl arms. The upper arm fits over the lower arm at the elbow. This enables the arm to bend at the elbow.) Some Cissy dolls do have one-piece arms that are not jointed at the elbow. The knees are jointed and most of the Cissy dolls are walkers.

Cissy came dressed in fashions that are a mirror of what the well dressed, sophisticated socialite of the 1950s would wear. A full range of fashions and accessories were available separately. The catalog advertised that lingerie, casual attire, sportswear, evening clothes, shoes, hosiery, millinery, and furs are available for Cissy. Chrome-plated clothes racks were sold by the company to hold her extensive wardrobe. Dozens of outfits were made and never pictured in the catalogs. Cissy was sold as a basic doll wearing a chemise and high heeled shoes called mules. Cissy walks, sits, and kneels. The catalog states "Cissy, the beautiful doll who has everything!"

1953
#1836, Winsome Winnie Walker, 18"
(Cissy)
Taffeta dress, cloth coat and hat, came with hat box with curlers, comb, and white gloves
$325.00 – 750.00

1954
#1875B, Sweet Violet, 18"
(Cissy)
Walking doll in a party dress, hat box with comb and curlers
$1,500.00 – 2,400.00

1954
#1835, Flower Girl, 18"
(Cissy)
Nylon net over taffeta dress, circlet of flowers in hair, hatbox contains curlers and comb
$550.00 – 1,000.00

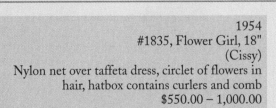

1955
#1818, Binnie, 18"
(Cissy)
Taffeta overdress over a white with red dot dress, came in three sizes, 15", 18", and 25".
$350.00 – 850.00

1955
#2097, Cissy, 20"
Blue satin gown with rhinestone decorations as well as silver and white braid trim
$1,500.00 – 2,200.00

1955
Cissy, 20"
Known by collectors as the Lucille Ball bride, very rare and desirable doll
$12,000.00+

1955
#2101, Cissy
Brocade bride gown decorated with pearls and rhinestones, tulle muff
$1,500.00 – 2,200.00

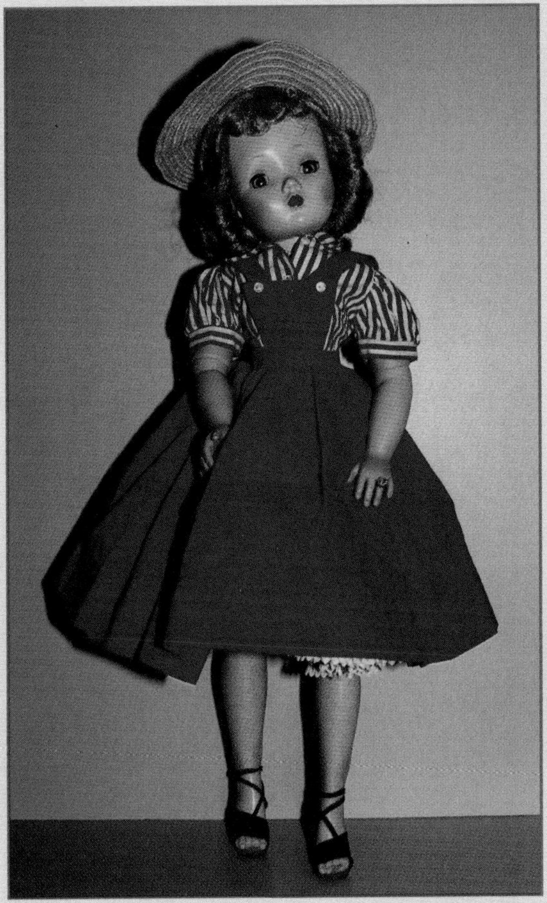

1955
#2083, Cissy, 20"
Red cotton dress and red striped blouse
$550.00 – 900.00

1955
#2100, Cissy, 20"
Mauve taffeta torso gown accented with a large taffeta bow
$1,500.00 – 2,200.00

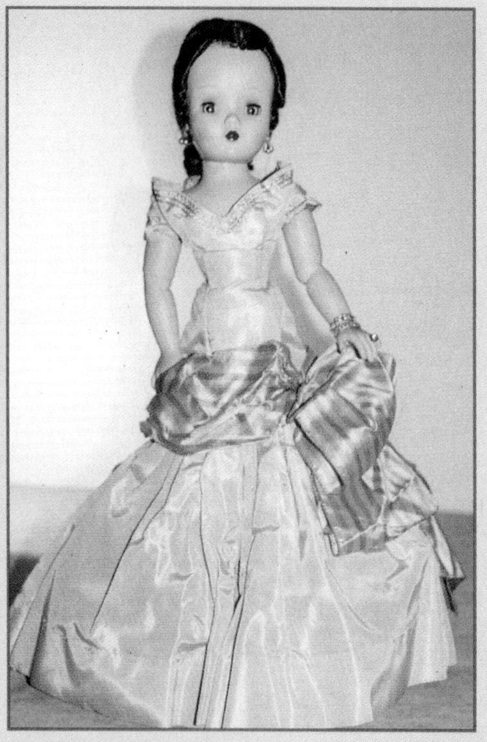

1955
#2100, Cissy, 20"
Same gown as in bottom photo page 119
with a different taffeta bow
$1,500.00 – 2,200.00

1955
#2094, Cissy, 20"
A Child's Dream Come True Collection
Heavy slipper satin gown with tulle muff with ruby red roses
$1,500.00 – 2,100.00

1956
#2027, Cissy, 20"
Checked circular skirt, white pique blouse
and bolero jacket
$800.00 – 1,500.00

1956
#2040, Cissy, 20"
Pleated tulle skirt, lace bodice over taffeta with loops of pearls at waist
$650.00 – 1,100.00

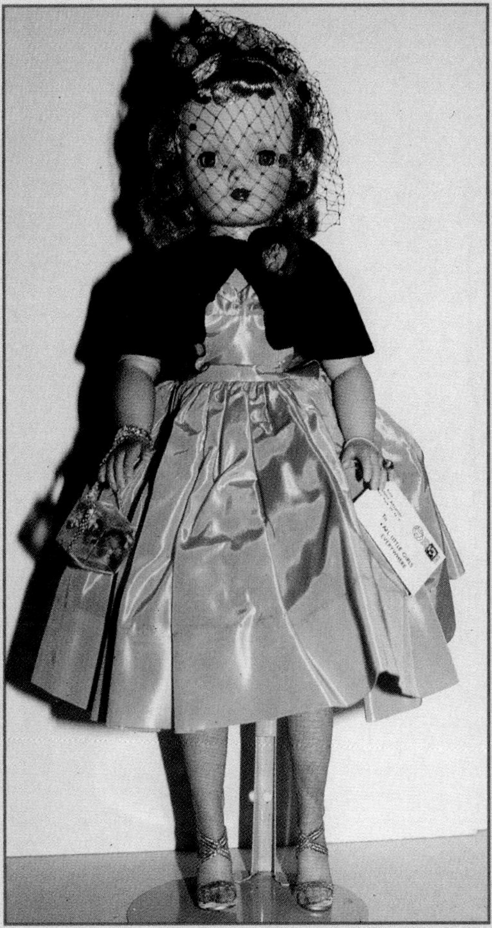

1956
#2017, Cissy, 20"
Taffeta dress with a black velvet jacket, tiny black velvet hat with flowers
$1,200.00 – 1,800.00

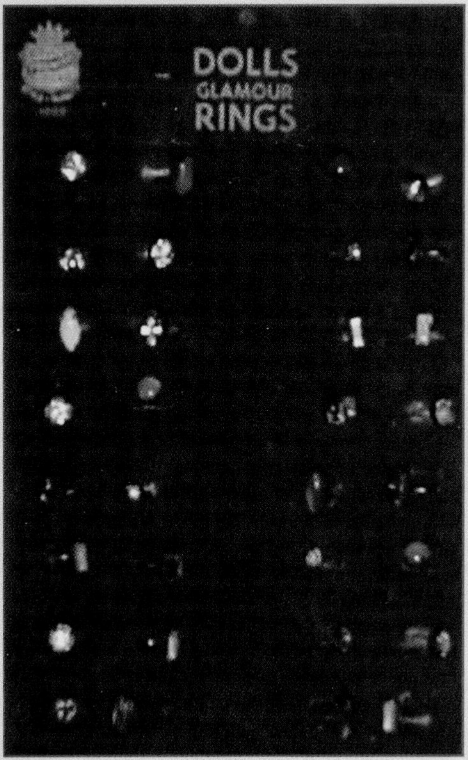

1950s
A stand up carboard display of rings of faux jewels for Cissy and Elise made by Premier Mint in package
$250.00

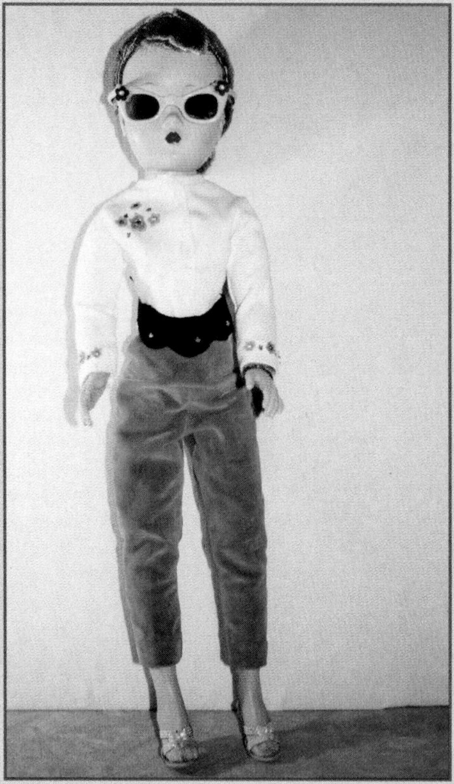

1956
#2007, Cissy, 20"
Velvet pants with a white cardigan top, ponytail hairdo
$1,500.00 – 2,200.00

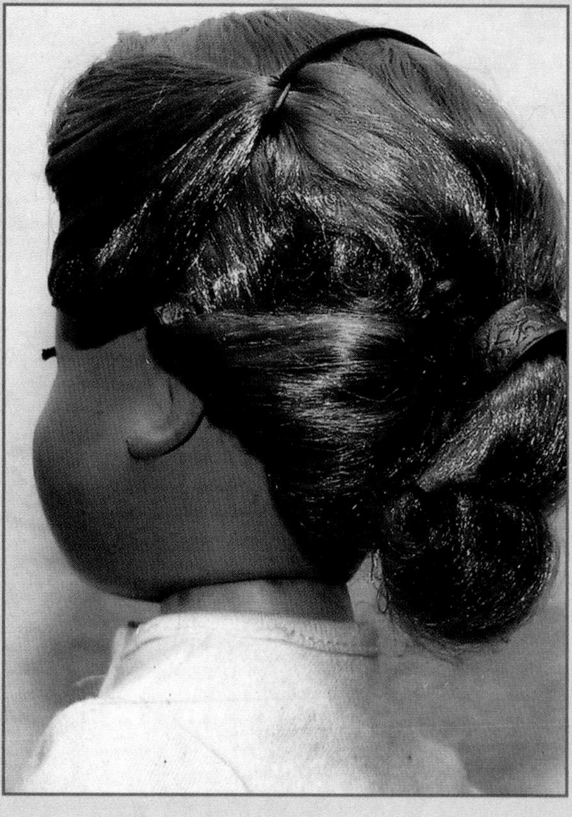

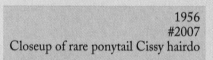

1956
#2007
Closeup of rare ponytail Cissy hairdo

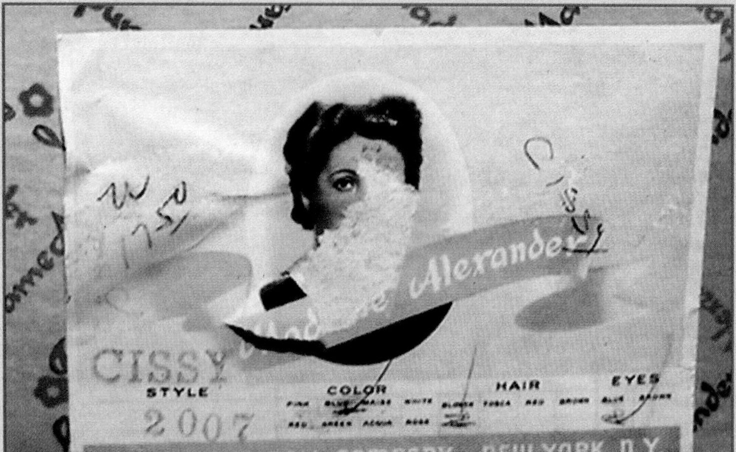

1956
#2007
Closeup of ponytail Cissy box

1956
#2020, Cissy, 20"
Gold satin theatre dress and matching coat
$700.00 – 1,200.00

1956
Cissy
Cotton print dress with navy blue straw hat with flowers
$750.00 – 1,200.00

1956
#2030, Cissy, 20"
Blue bridesmaid dress with tulle over satin,
tulle hat with flowers on each side
$700.00 – 1,000.00

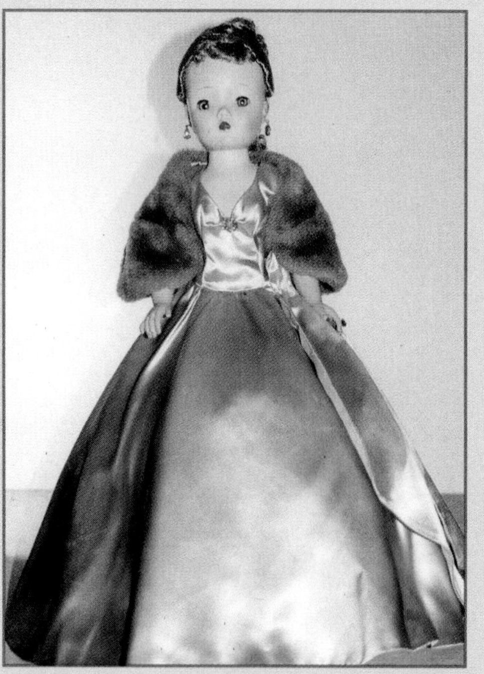

1956
#2041, Cissy, 20"
Orlon fur stole worn over a blue satin evening gown
$1,500.00 – 2,100.00

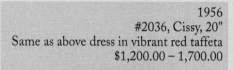

1956
#2036, Cissy, 20"
Same as above dress in vibrant red taffeta
$1,200.00 – 1,700.00

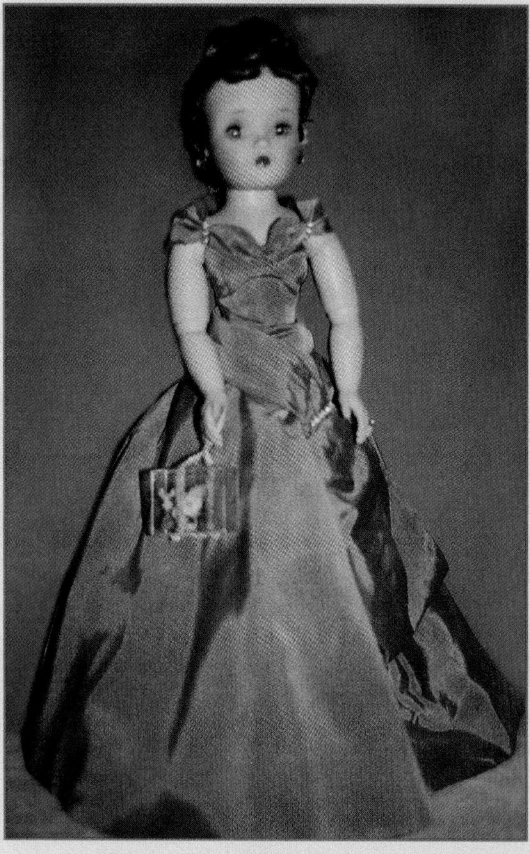

1956
#2036, Cissy, 20"
Pink taffeta evening gown with rhinestone pin holding sash in place
$1,500.00 – 2,200.00

1957
#2175, Lady Hamilton, 20"
(Cissy)
Blue silk gown with a large rose attached to the front of her stole
Not mint
$800.00 – 1,400.00

1956
#2043, Cissy, 20"
Black velvet torso gown trimmed with pink roses at the shoulder and top of tulle flounce
Mint
$1,200.00 – 1,800.00

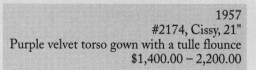

1957
#2174, Cissy, 21"
Purple velvet torso gown with a tulle flounce
$1,400.00 – 2,200.00

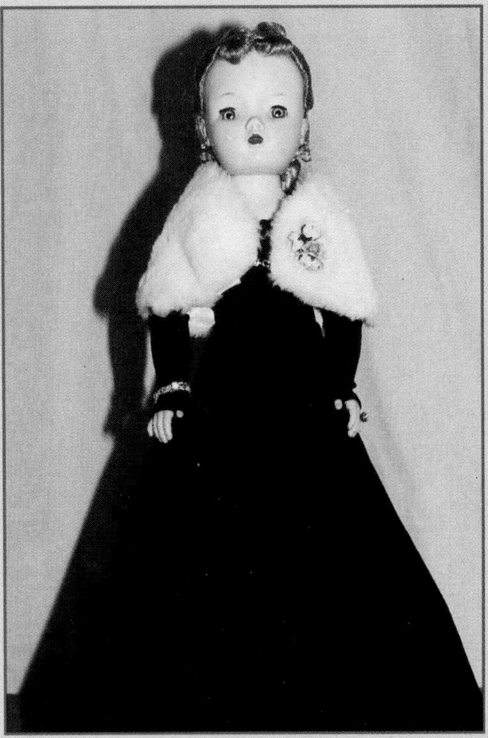

1957
#2173, Cissy, 20"
Orlon fur stole, black velvet gown
$800.00 – 1,200.00

1957
#2160, Cissy, 20"
Dotted nylon gown with pink taffeta underskirt, flowered trimmed hat
$1,800.00 – 2,800.00

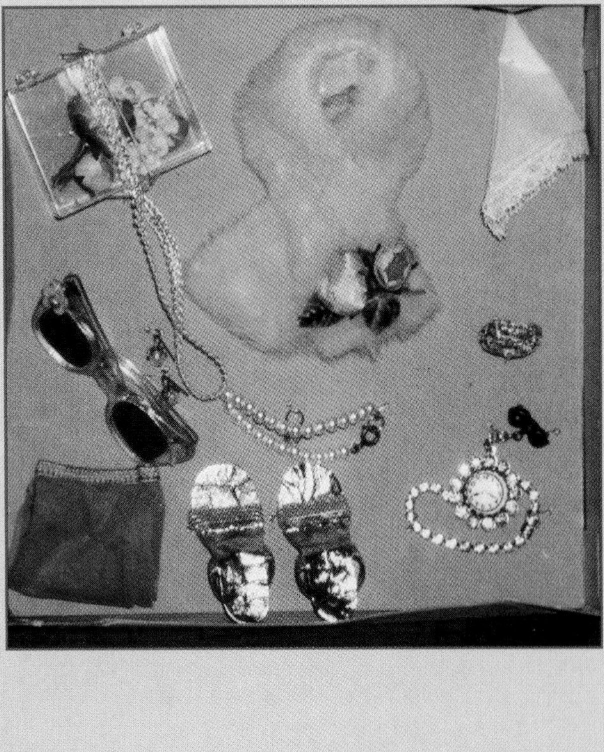

1957
Accessories for Cissy
$395.00

1957
#2120, Cissy, 20"
Yellow dress with cameo, large black hat
Mint
$1,200.00 – 1,800.00

1957
#2141, Cissy, 20"
Navy taffeta dress with ruffled organdy cape, lacy straw hat trimmed with flowers
$1,200.00 – 1,900.00

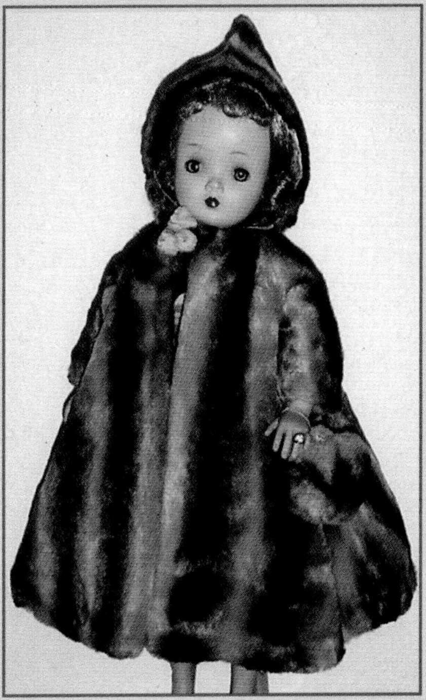

1957
Cissy, 20"
Orlon coat, hat, and muff that was available as a boxed outfit
Boxed outfit, $450.00

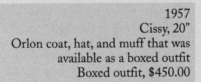

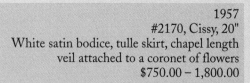

1957
#2176, Cissy, 20"
Blue taffeta gown with straw hat with flowers
$800.00 – 1,300.00

1957
#2170, Cissy, 20"
White satin bodice, tulle skirt, chapel length veil attached to a coronet of flowers
$750.00 – 1,800.00

1958
#2280, Cissy, 20"
Bridal gown with intricate embroidered wreath pattern on skirt, full length tulle veil attached to a coronet of flowers
Very rare brown eyes were authenticated by the company
$3,000.00

1958
#2252, Cissy, 20"
Satin dress with tulle stole
$1,500.00 – 2,100.00

1958
#2142, Cissy, 20"
Organdy dress, pink sash
$800.00 – 1,600.00

1958
#2283, Camellia, 20"
(Cissy)
Silk ball gown, velvet stole, hoop slip underneath
$1,500.00 – $2,400.00

1958
#2282, Cissy, 20"
Tulle evening gown flocked with flowers, original horsehair hat
Mint
$1,500.00 – 2,200.00

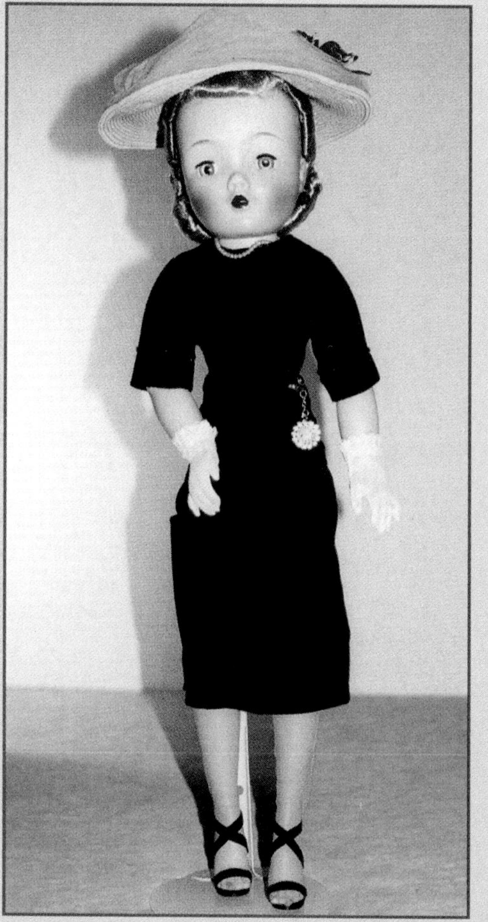

1958
Cissy, 20"
Black velvet dress, blue hat, extremely rare doll
$1,500.00 – 2,400.00

1958
Cissy, 20"
Blue taffeta shirtwaist dress with straw hat, uncataloged
$1,200.00 – 1,900.00

1958
#2285, Cissy, 20"
Red taffeta dress, tulle stole covers hair and drapes to the hem of dress, unique hairdo
$1,800.00 – 2,600.00

1958
Left: #2222, Cissy, 20"
Right: #2235
Cotton dresses with straw hats
$550.00 – 900.00 each

1959
#2150, Cissy, 20"
Satin dress with matching stole, tulle hat trimmed with flowers
Rare
$1,500.00 – 2,600.00

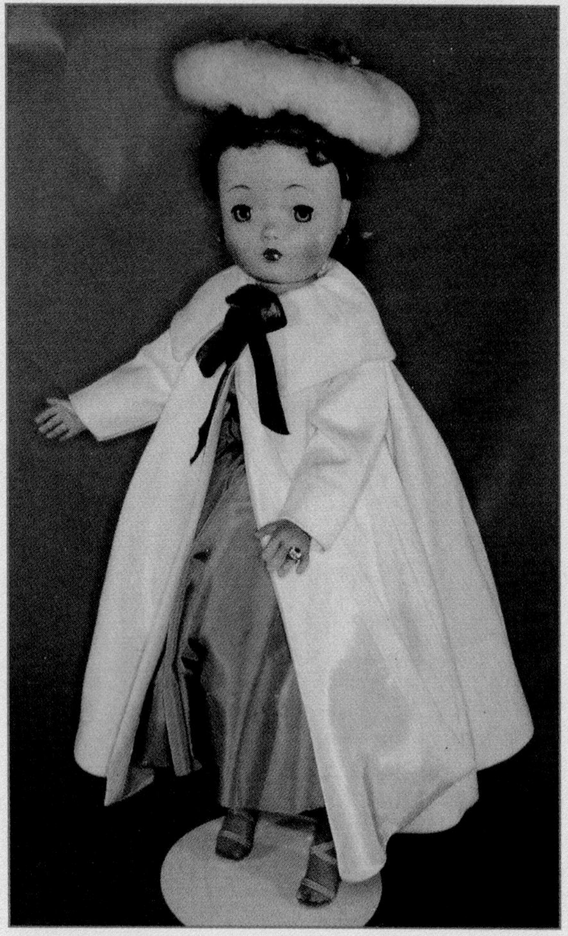

1959
#2118, Cissy, 20"
White taffeta coat, taffeta dress, and fur hat
$850.00 – 1,500.00

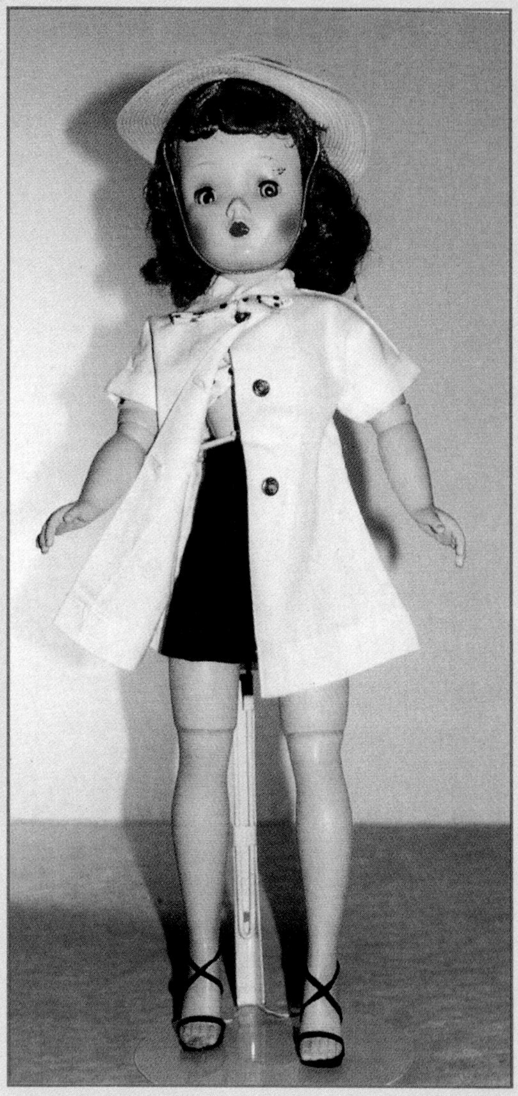

Cissy, 20"
Navy shorts, navy dotted top with white coverup
$850.00 – 1,500.00

Cissy, 20"
Boxed outfit with cotton bathing suit with matching skirt
Boxed outfit, $550.00

Late 1950s
Cissy, 20"
Red velvet coat, straw hat
$850.00 – 1,500.00

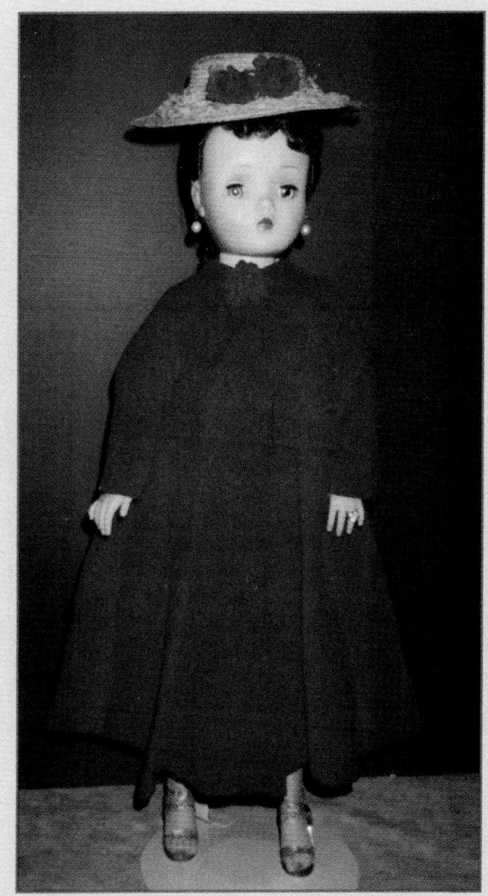

Cissy, 20"
Cotton dress with organdy sleeves
$650.00 – 900.00

Cissy, 20", hard plastic
Original pegnoir set
$650.00 – 900.00

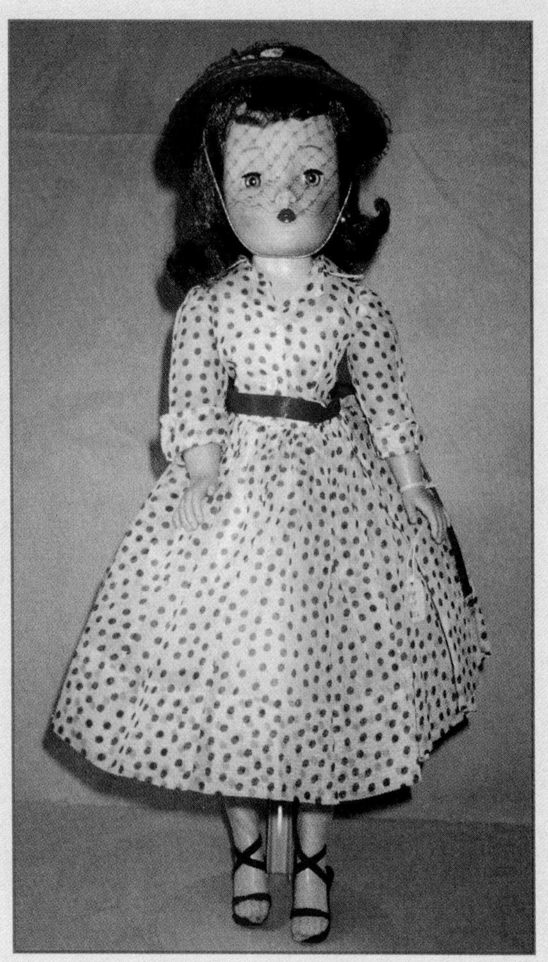

#2019
Cissy, 20"
Red dotted organdy dress with red sash at waist, red straw hat with flower trim
$650.00 – 1,000.00

Late 1950s
Tulle evening gown
$1,500.00 – 2,200.00

Late 1950s
Cissy, 20"
Variation of dress in red
$1,600.00 – 2,400.00

Late 1950s
Cissy, 20"
Blue brocade dress and matching stole
$1,500.00 – 2,400.00

Late 1950s
Cissy, 20"
Satin cocktail dress
$1,200.00 – 1,800.00

Late 1950s
Cissy, 20"
Classic suit with rhinestone pin and belt buckle
$650.00 – 1,000.00

1960
Red evening gown of dotted tulle over organdy
$1,200.00 – 1,900.00

1960
Cissy, 20"
Boxed outfit, flowered skirt, white top
Boxed outfit, $400.00

1961
#2230,Queen Elizabeth
Brocade gown with sash of the garter, extra long eyelashes
$1,200.00 – 1,900.00

1961
Cissy, 20"
Rare tulle evening gown with a cascade of flowers
$1,500.00 – 2,400.00

1961
#2245, Lissy Cissy
Mauve pleated tulle dress trimmed with sequins
$1,300.00 – 2,100.00

1961
#2240, Cissy Scarlett
Blue taffeta outfit with black braid trim
All hard plastic with one-piece arms
$1,400.00 – 2,100.00

1961
Renoir
Satin ballgown and jacket
$1,200.00 – 1,800.00

1961
#2235, Cissy Melanie, 20"
Blue satin dress with elaborate
Godey hairdo, lace coat
$1,300.00 – 2,000.00

1961
Scarlett Portrait, 20"
(Cissy)
Mint and all original
$1,500.00 – 2,400.00

1961
An uncataloged doll, which collectors have thought was Godey or Melanie.
Wrist tag and tag in outfit both state Cissy
$1,600.00 – 2,500.00

1962
#2170
(Cissy)
Very elaborate gown of lace over pleated tulle, very rare doll
$1,500.00 – 2,100.00

1962
#2260, Cissy Godey
Orange gown with matching velvet jacket, natural straw hat with big pink roses
$1,500.00 – 2,100.00

Coronation Set

Abraham and Straus, a large Brooklyn department store, approached Madame Alexander in 1952 about making a set of dolls representing the Coronation of Queen Elizabeth II. Madame Alexander researched the clothing, fabrics, jewelry, the crowns as well as the people involved in the coronation. The detail on the set is spectacular. Abraham and Straus made an elaborate setting appropriate for the coronation. The huge set was on display at Abraham and Straus and was shown on TV by CBS. The set was later donated to the Brooklyn Children's Museum. My deepest thanks to Nancy Paine of the Brooklyn Children's Museum for giving permission for me to photograph and share this one-of-a-kind wonderful coronation set with collectors. The Coronation set is one of a kind therefore no prices are shown.

1952
Queen in Recessional, 18"
(Margaret)
Purple velvet cornation robe trimmed in ermine, gold chain with seven medals is draped around her shoulders

1952
Queen in Processional, 18"
(Margaret)
Red velvet robe trimmed in ermine, over a satin dress decorated in gold
She wore this for the processional from Buckingham Palace to Westminster Abbey.

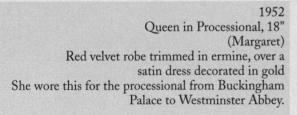

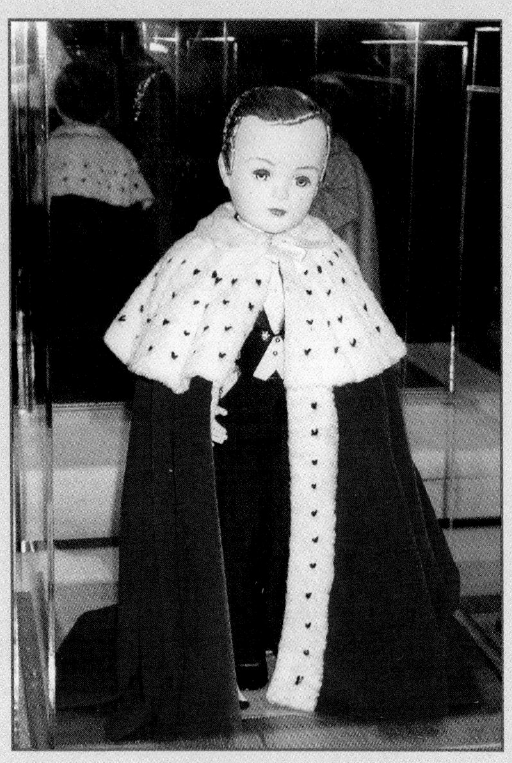

1952
Duke of Edinburgh, 21"
(Margaret)
Crimson velvet robe over formal navy uniform

1952
Queen Mother, 18"
(Margaret)
White brocade gown embroidered with jewels, purple velvet robe trimmed in ermine

1952
Princess Margaret, 18"
(Margaret)
White gown adorned with jewels under a purple velvet robe, trimmed in ermine, two diamond bracelets, earrings, necklace, and tiara

1952
Prince Charles, 11"
(Precious Toddler)
Linen pants and a silk shirt with lace at the collar and cuffs

1952
Privy Councillor's Lady, 18"
(Margaret)
Lace gown decorated with diamonds under a red velvet layered robe, red velvet bag trimmed in gold

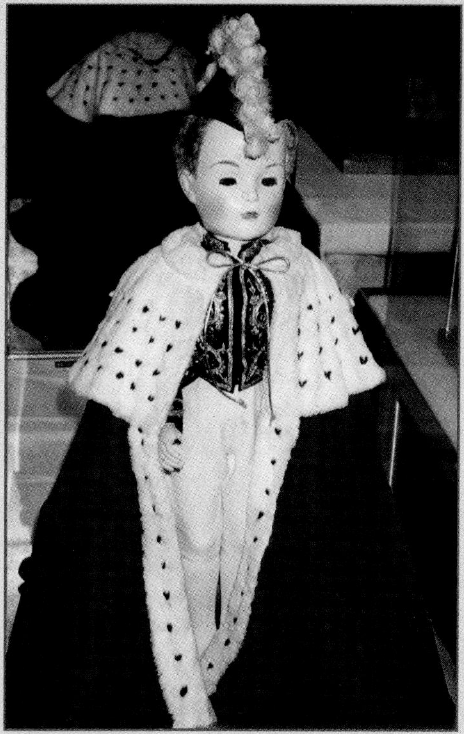

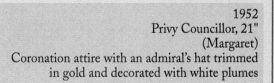

1952
Privy Councillor, 21"
(Margaret)
Coronation attire with an admiral's hat trimmed in gold and decorated with white plumes

1952
Coronation Ball Dancer, 18"
(Margaret)
Ballgown embroidered in gold, gold necklace, earrings, and tiara

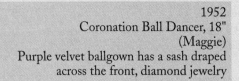

1952
Coronation Ball Dancer, 18"
(Maggie)
Purple velvet ballgown has a sash draped across the front, diamond jewelry

1952
Coronation Ball Dancer, 18"
(Winnie)
Black velvet gown decorated with sequins to form a leaf design, two bracelets, gold earrings, and tiara

1952
Coronation Ball Dancer
(Margaret)
Pink ballgown embroidered with gold and jewels, gold tiara of rubies and three bracelets

1952
Coronation Ball Dancer, 18"
(Maggie)
Gown has a striped panel down the side, diamond and star sash drapes across the gown, diamond tiara

1952
Coronation Ball Dancer, 18"
(Margaret)
Chiffon gown has a gold skirt underneath, bodice is accented with pearls and aquamarines

1952
Maid of Honor: Lady Rosemary Spencer Churchill, 18" (Margaret)
Silver dress accented on the bodice with pearls, tiara and earrings are made of pearls

1952
Maid of Honor: Lady Moyra Hamilton, 18" (Maggie)
Lamé gown decorated with pearls on the bodice, pearl necklace, and tiara

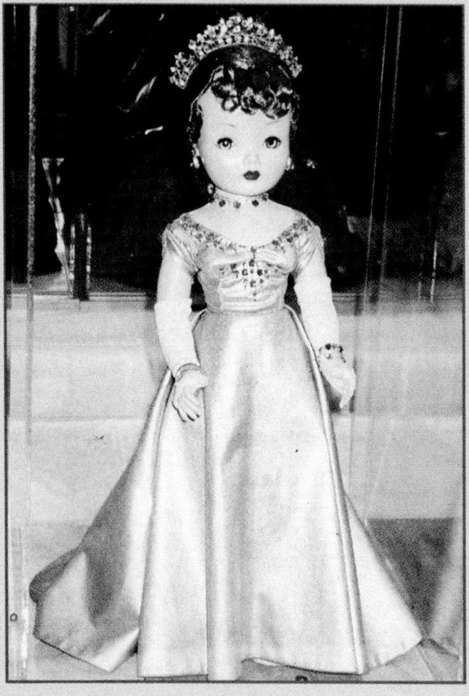

1952
Maid of Honor: Lady Jane Vane-Tempest-Stewart, 18" (Winnie)
Silver lamé dress with a bodice sprinkled with diamonds

1952
Maid of Honor:
Lady Jane Heathcote-Drummond-Willoughby, 18"
(Margaret)
Bodice is accented with diamond and ruby pendants

1952
Maid of Honor: Lady Mary Baillie-Hamilton, 18"
(Winnie)
Gown has amber drops and green jewels on the bodice

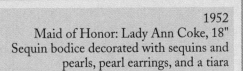

1952
Maid of Honor: Lady Ann Coke, 18"
Sequin bodice decorated with sequins and pearls, pearl earrings, and a tiara

1952
Choir Boys, 14"
(two Margaret, one Winnie, and two Maggie)
White linen cloaks over felt jackets and black trousers, music booklet

1952
Marquis of Salisbury, 21"
(Margaret)
White trousers, felt jacket, and crimson velvet robe edged in ermine, jeweled sword of state

1952
Duke of Gordon, 21"
(Margaret)
White trousers, felt jacket, and a crimson robe trimmed in ermine, Queen's ring on a red velvet cushion

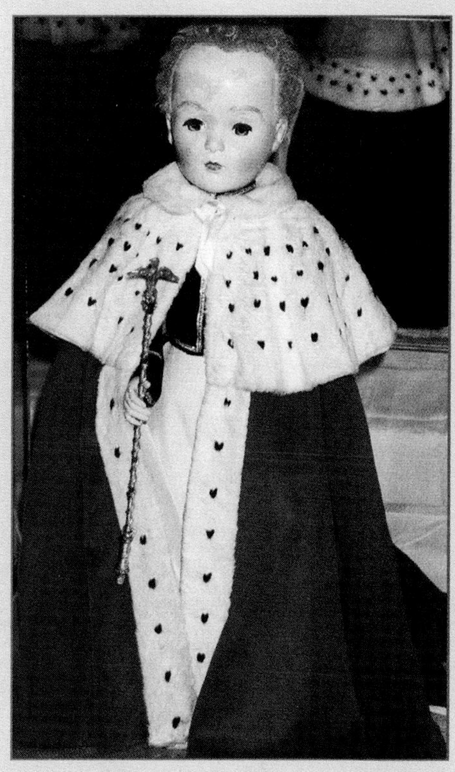

1952
Duke of Richmond, 21"
(Margaret)
Clothing is similiar to the Duke of Gordon,
scepter with the dove pledges equal justice

1952
Earl of Alexander, 21"
(Maggie)
Dressed the same as the Duke of Gordon,
Royal Orb on a red velvet cushion

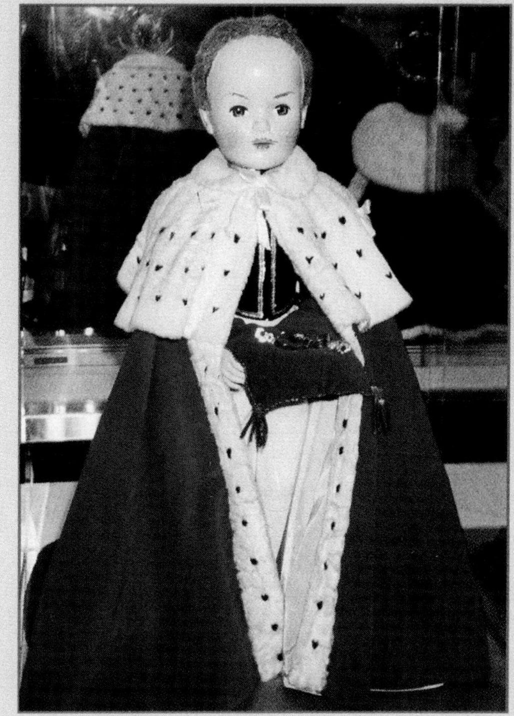

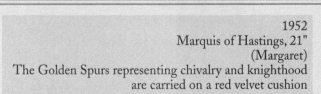

1952
Marquis of Hastings, 21"
(Margaret)
The Golden Spurs representing chivalry and knighthood
are carried on a red velvet cushion

The 16½" Elise is made of hard plastic with joints at the knees, ankles, and elbows. She was made in this size from 1957 to 1961, 17" in 1962, and 18" in 1963 and 1964. The catalog reveals that with the jointed ankles, Elise can wear high or low heels. She can sit, walk, or kneel. The arms are made of vinyl. Elise was available as a dressed doll or as a basic doll with clothes that could be purchased separately. In 1966 the Alexander Company introduced a new mold for Elise with a more slender body of rigid plastic and a vinyl head.

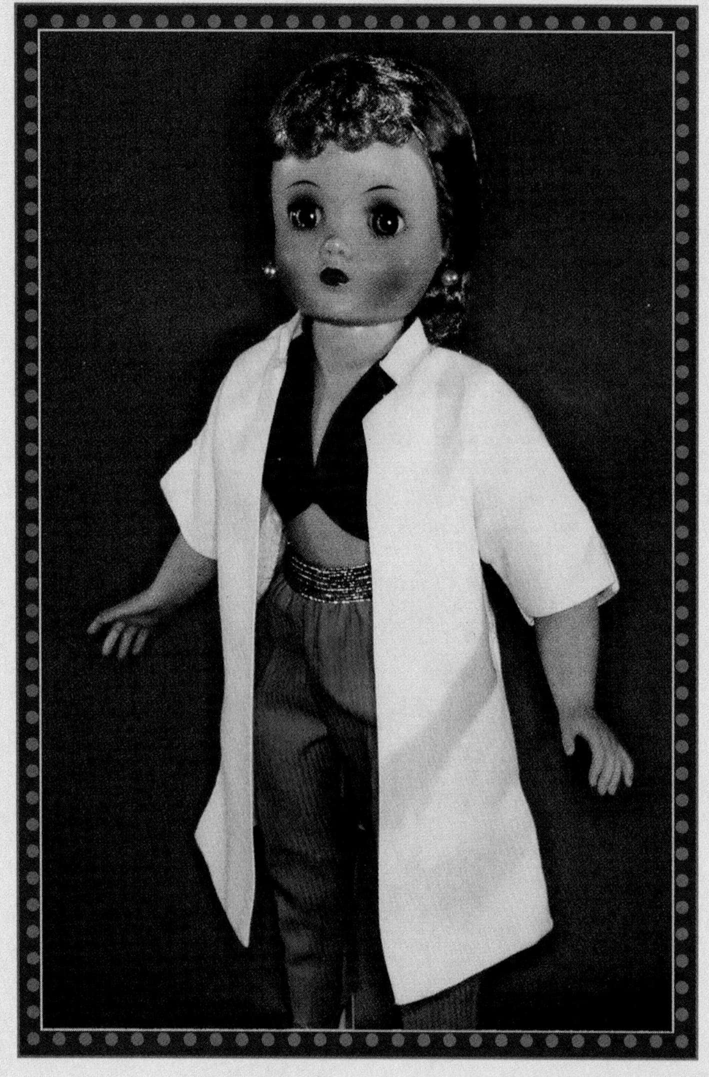

1958
Elise
Rare uncataloged outfit, tagged, matches both Cissy and Cissette from 1958
$500.00 – 775.00

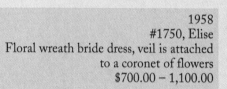

1958
#1750, Elise
Floral wreath bride dress, veil is attached to a coronet of flowers
$700.00 – 1,100.00

1958
#1718, Elise
Nylon dress trimmed in val lace and tiny buttons
$475.00 – 950.00

1959
#1830, Elise Bridesmaid
Pleated nylon with flowers on bodice and waist, large hat with flowers
$800.00 – 1,100.00

1958
Elise
Shirtdress of cotton print, handbag, earrings, and a ring
Identical outfits made for 20" Cissy and 10" Cissette
$500.00 – 975.00

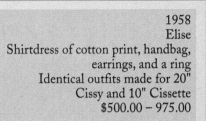

1959
#1810, Elise Ballerina, 16½"
Gold cloth top with gold net tutu, sequin tiara
$400.00 – 750.00

1959
#1835, Elise
Rare pink nylon tulle bride gown, veil attached to a coronet of flowers
$625.00 – 995.00

1960
#1735, Elise
White satin bride gown, tulle is attached to a coronet of flowers
$525.00 – 1,100.00

1963
#1780, Elise as Queen Elizabeth
Brocade gown with the sash of the order of the Bath
$750.00 – 1,100.00

1963
#1710, Elise
Riding clothes complete with boots and cap
$425.00 – 850.00

1962
Elise, 17"
Godey style outfit made for FAO Schwarz
$750.00 – 1,100.00

1963
#1720, Elise Ballerina
All original
$400.00 – 750.00

1963
#1715
Elise body and Marybel head
Made in 1963 only
$500.00 – 850.00

1964
#1740, Elise Bride, 18"
Wedding gown of tiers of lace and chapel length veil
$475.00 – 950.00

Jacqueline

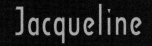

The 21" Jacqueline face doll was first made in 1961. She has a fully jointed hard plastic body, and vinyl head and arms. There can be little doubt that this doll was fashioned after Jacqueline Kennedy, the wife of President John Kennedy who was elected in 1960. In the 1962 catalog Jacqueline and Caroline dolls are shown together in a picture with a rack of clothes that could be purchased for the dolls. Mrs. Kennedy always wore the height of fashion and the country was enchanted with her clothes and lifestyle. In the catalogs the name Kennedy is not mentioned. Jacqueline was made in 1960 and 1961 in a variety of outfits from elegant evening gowns, dresses, and suits to a riding outfit. In 1962, the Cissette face was made as Jacqueline with a dark wig with a curl on the forehead. In 1965, the Alexander company began using the Jacqueline dolls for their portrait dolls. The first portrait dolls made with the Jacqueline doll were Scarlett, Southern Belle, Renoir, Godey, Bride, and Queen. Portrait dolls with the Jacqueline face became a regular part of the Alexander line.

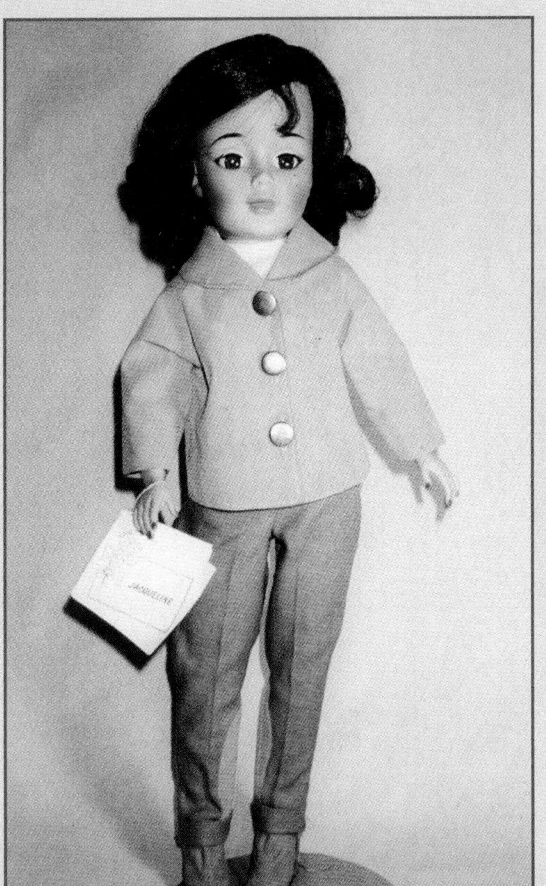

1962
#2117, Jacqueline, 21"
Riding clothes, all original with wrist tag
$900.00 – 1,500.00.

1965
#2152, Scarlett, 21"
(Jacqueline)
Emerald green satin dress with lace and black velvet ribbon at neckline
$1,500.00 – 2,200.00

1965
#2151
Jacqueline Bride, 21"
Satin bridal gown with veil attached to a coronet of flowers
$750.00 – 1,200.00

1962
#2130, Jacqueline Kennedy, 21"
(Jacqueline)
Brocade evening gown
$850.00 – 1,500.00

Janie

Janie is 12" tall and has a toddler body and legs of plastic with a vinyl head and arms. She was made as Janie only from 1964 to 1966 but was made later with the same face and body as Rozy, Suzy, Lucinda, and Gretl, Frederick, and Marta of *The Sound of Music*. In 1964, Janie was offered in five different outfits, in 1965, she was offered in four outfits, and in 1966 only two outfits were offered.

The Janie face and body was used as the black Katie in 1965 only. Katie came in two outfits only.

1965
#1124, Janie Ballerina, 12"
All original
$250.00 – 450.00

1964
Janie, 12"
All original
Matching 8" BK Walker Wendy
Outfit also made for 18" Binnie
12" Janie, $275.00 – 450.00
8" Wendy, $375.00 – 750.00

1964
Left: #1157, Janie
White pique dress missing pen and notebook
$275.00 – 425.00
Right: #1158, Janie, 12"
Linen dress
$225.00 – 400.00

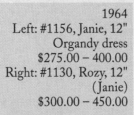

1964
Left: #1156, Janie, 12"
Organdy dress
$275.00 – 400.00
Right: #1130, Rozy, 12"
(Janie)
$300.00 – 450.00

1964
#1162, Janie, 12" (standing)
Unusual red coat and hat, plastic/vinyl
$300.00 – 450.00
Smarty (sitting)
Original outfit from 1964, plastic/vinyl
$275.00 – 400.00

Lissy

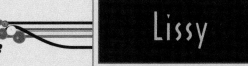

The 11½" to 12" doll was made from 1956 to 1958. She was made of all hard plastic with joints at the knees and elbows. Her feet are slightly arched to wear sandals with hose or white socks. Lissy has a glued-on wig and is not marked anywhere on her body. Only her clothes are tagged. Dressed dolls were sold as well as many boxed outfits. The basic Lissy could be purchased in her chemise and shoes. A number of 8" dolls were made with identical outfits to Lissy. The 8" dolls are pictured in the catalogs while many of the Lissys are not. The matching outfits do help to date when the Lissys were made. The 1957 and 1958 Little Women wore white socks and black sandals.

Between 1959 and 1967, Lissy dolls were made with the Lissy head but on a body with no joints at the elbows or knees. The feet were flat. During this time the Lissy face Little Women were made.

In 1959, Kelly was made in a variety of outfits with the Lissy face but with no joints at the knees and elbows. She was made of all hard plastic with a glued-on wig.

Pamela was made in 1962 with the Lissy face and body with no joints at the knees and elbows. Pamela came with three interchangeable wigs in a gift set with extra clothing. The wigs attached to a Velcro strip on her head. Pamela was also made with the later Nancy Drew vinyl head.

In 1962, the Lissy face Tommy and Katie were made for FAO Schwarz's 100th anniversary.

In 1963, the Classics Group composed of Scarlett O'Hara, Southern Belle, and McGuffey Ana were made with the Lissy face.

Brigitta of the large set of *The Sound of Music* was made in 1965 in the sailor outfit and the Alpine outfit using the Lissy face.

1956
#1247
Bride gown of lace and pleated tulle with pink satin sash at waist
$650.00 – 1,000.00

1956
#1226
Lined circular skirt, sheer organdy blouse, and red velvet bonnet
$400.00 – 725.00

1956
Polished yellow cotton dress with white organdy pinafore
$375.00 – 750.00

1956
#1242
Nylon tulle tutu with satin bodice
$475.00 – 850.00

1956
#1222
Polished cotton dress with
white pique Danish bonnet
$350.00 – 700.00

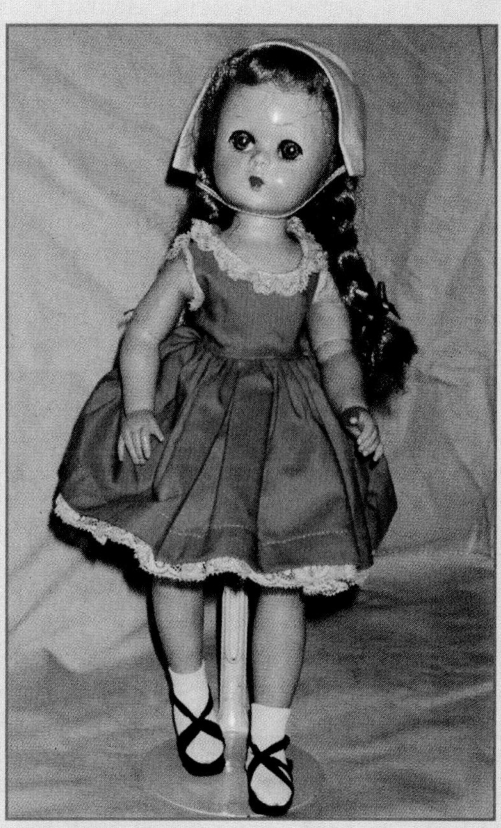

1956
#1247
Nylon tulle dancing dress
$700.00 – 1,200.00

1956
#1248
Nylon tulle bridesmaid's dress
with a satin sash
$750.00 – 1,500.00

1956
#1250
Dressed for an afternoon party in a taffeta dress and tulle hat, Baby Louis sandals
$475.00 – 900.00

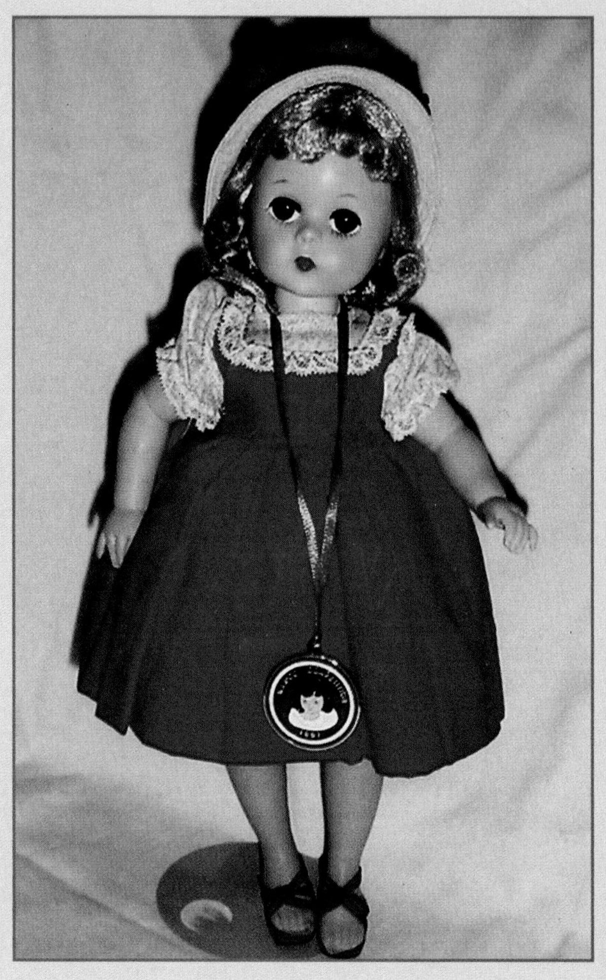

1956 – 1958
Print dress and cotton pinafore, uncataloged
$450.00 – 850.00

1956
Cotton dress with a taffeta pinafore and hat
$425.00 – 800.00

1957
#1190
Marme of Little Women
Polished cotton dress
$350.00 – 650.00

1957
#1190, Meg of Little Women
Polished cotton dress, Baby Louis elastic sandals
$350.00 – 600.00

1957
Pinafore worn over organdy pinafore, shown on clothes rack in 1957 catalog reprints
$525.00 – 850.00

1957
Taffeta basic dress
$400.00 – 800.00

1957
Carcoat set, very rare
$600.00 – 1,000.00

1957
#1161
Rare version in green
$700.00 – 1,200.00

1957
#1161
Ankle-length bridesmaid's dress of nylon with val lace trim
$600.00 – 1,000.00

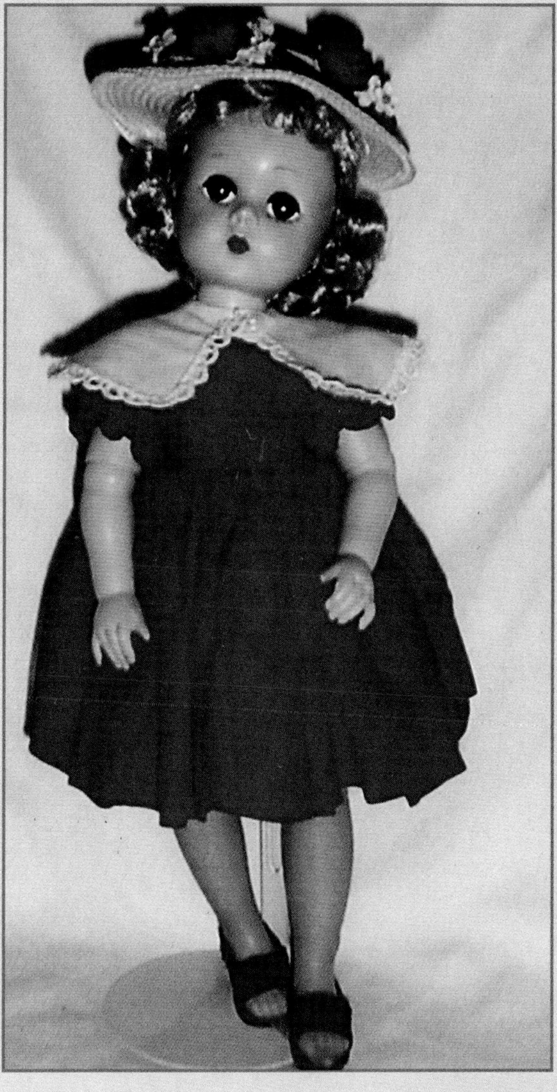

1957
#1151
Red taffeta dress with white Quaker collar, straw hat with flowers
$500.00 – 850.00

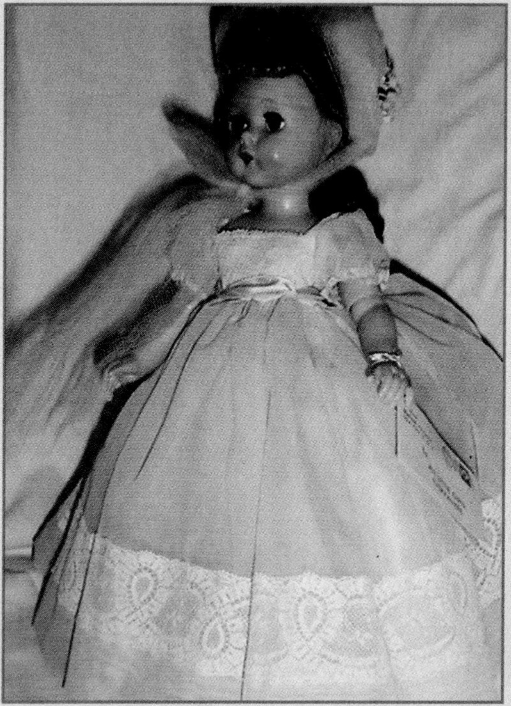

1957
#1161
Rare lavender bridesmaid's dress
$550.00 – 950.00

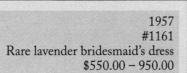

1957
#1151
Rare blue taffeta version
$600.00 – 950.00

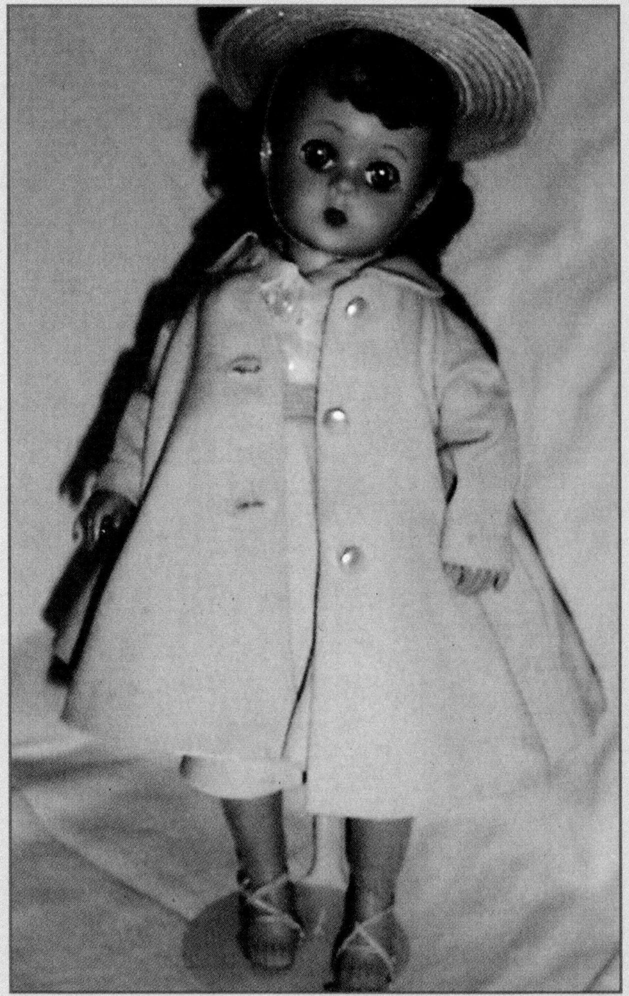

1957
Lissy gift set, pink circular skirt and coat, nylon blouse, and straw hat
$475.00 – 750.00

1957
Lissy Graduation
Swiss dotted organdy with blue ribbon sash, original diploma
$700.00 – 1,500.00

1958
#1225, Amy of Little Women
Cotton dress with organdy collar
$350.00 – 650.00

1958
#1225, Beth of Little Women
Notice the Baby Louis sandals that came on Little Women, 1956 – 1958
$ 375.00 – 700.00

1958
#1218
Ready for almost any occasion, checked dress with cotton pinafore, missing hat
$375.00 – 750.00

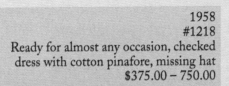

1956 – 1958
Rare dress and cotton pinafore, uncataloged
$550.00 – 900.00

1959
#1103, Kelly
Lace-trimmed nylon dress with satin sash, earrings
$700.00 – 950.00

1959
#1110, Kelly
Sheer nylon dress trimmed with val lace, wide ribbon sash with corsage of flowers
$600.00 – 1,000.00

1959
#1103, Kelly, 12"
(Lissy)
Nylon print dress with ribbon sash
Came in blue, yellow, and pink
$425.00 – 850.00

1959
#1102, Kelly
Checked cotton dress with polished cotton pinafore
$425.00 – 800.00

1959
#1105, Kelly
Cotton dress with straw hat
$400.00 – 850.00

1959
Lissy and Wendy Amy
Print dress with polished cotton pinafore
Lissy, $350.00 – 600.00
Wendy, $300.00 – 500.00

1959
Kelly
Cotton dress and organdy pinafore
$450.00 – 950.00

Early 1960s
Little Women, 12"
(Lissy)
Hard plastic
$275.00 – 500.00 each

1961
#1225
Meg of Little Women
Lavender striped cotton dress, black side snap shoes
$275.00 – 450.00

1962 only
FAO Schwarz Katie and Tommy
(Lissy)
Yellow taffeta dress, velvet ribbon,
cotton suit with white collar
$650.00 – 950.00 each

1962
#1225, Beth of Little Women
Checked cotton dress, eyelet pinafore, black side snap shoes
$275.00 – 500.00

1963
#1256, Scarlett O'Hara of the Classics Group
Green taffeta dress and bonnet
$900.00 – 1,500.00

1963
#1255, Southern Belle of the Classics Group
Taffeta dress trimmed in lace, straw hat with flowers
$900.00 – 1,500.00

Closeup of 1963 Southern Belle

1963
#1258, McGuffey Ana of the Classics Group
Red velvet suit, fur hat, collar, and mittens, patent leather slippers, and buttoned gaitors, very rare doll
$2,700.00

1963
#1225, Marme of Little Women
$300.00 – 500.00

1962
#1290, Pamela
Magenta taffeta skirt with organdy top, blonde wig
$375.00

1962
#1290, Pamela, 12"
(Lissy)
Polished cotton outfit from the gift case
$375.00

1963
#1285, Pamela
Pink taffeta dress
$350.00

1964
Lissy Italian prototype
Has cloth hat instead of straw hat
one-of-a-kind

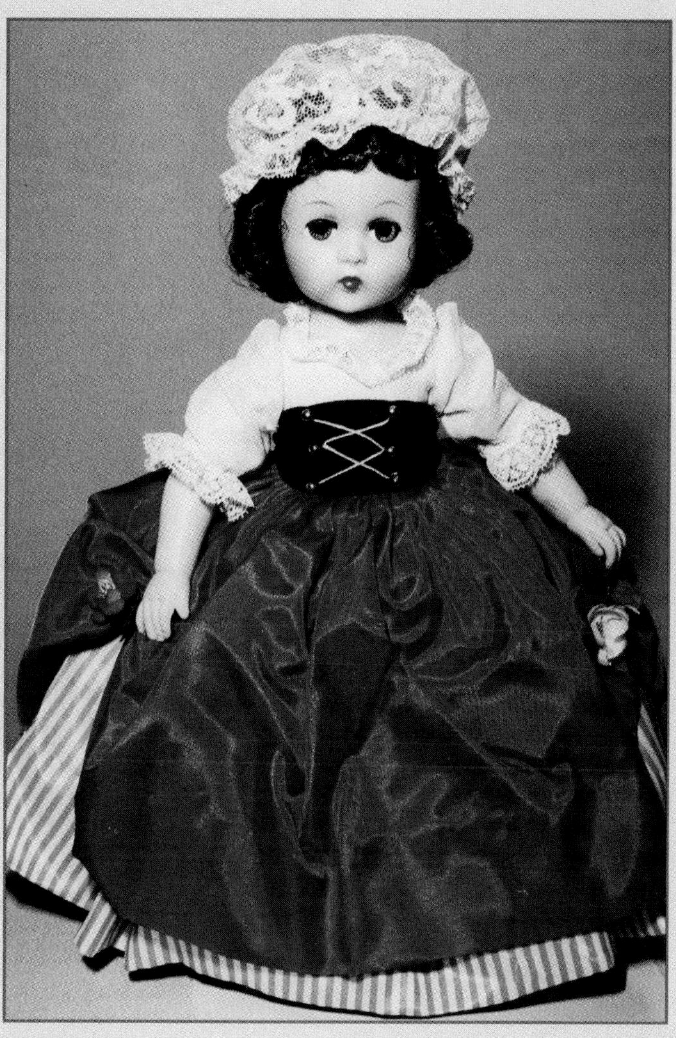

Probably 1964
Lissy French prototype
one-of-a-kind

1964
Polish Lissy prototype
Matches 8" Polish of 1964
one-of-a-kind

1965
Mary Ellen Playmate
(Lissy)
FAO Schwarz exclusive gift set
$1,200.00

1965
Brigitta of *The Sound of Music*
(Lissy)
Rare sailor outfit
$450.00 – 750.00

1965
Marme of Little Women
Cotton dress, eyelet apron
$275.00 – 425.00

Little Genius

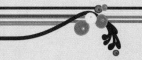

Madame Alexander formally introduced Little Genius in her 1956 line. The 1956 booklet states "Little Genius, our new drinking and wetting baby, 8" tall. Jointed vinyl body, saran wig. Goes to sleep. Basic baby wears training pants and matching bonnet with ribbon trimmed booties." Little Genius had a hard plastic head with a small hole for nursing. Booklets show that a bottle came with each Little Genius and some came with spoons. She often came with crocheted booties with pink elastic around the ankle decorated with pink flower attached by a metal brad. A large variety of outfits were available for purchase to make Little Genius a very well dressed baby.

The Little Genius head actually first appeared on the hard plastic Quiz-kin body when the Quiz-kin Christening Baby was made in 1953. In 1954, the Little Genius hard plastic head was used on a one piece latex body that had no joints at the hip or shoulder. Wendy-kin baby is often found in eyelet covered plastic pants that are tagged "Wendy-kin." They also were sold in dresses and baby outfits. Some of the dolls had the caracul hair.

1953
#318, Quiz-kin Christening Baby, 8"
(Little Genius)
$325.00 – 750.00

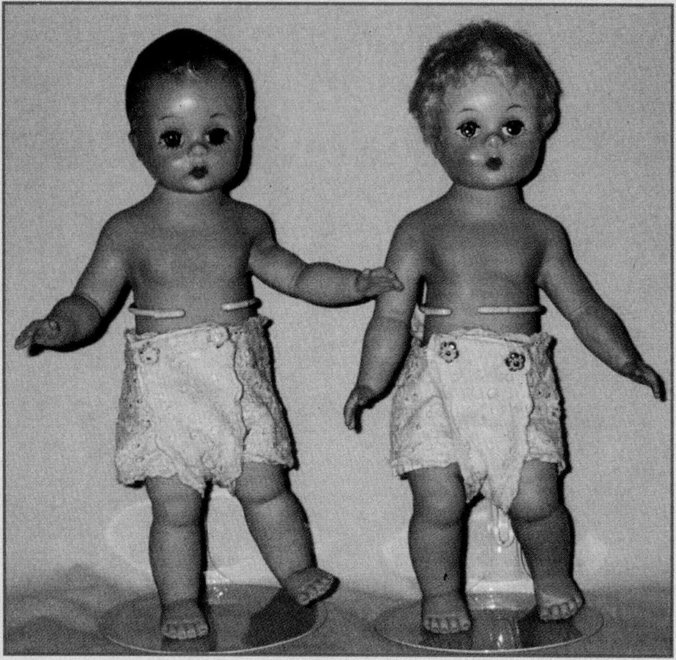

1954
Wendy-kin Babies, 8"
(Little Genius)
One-piece latex bodies
The eyelet covered plastic pants are tagged "Wendy-kin"
The left one has a painted head, while the right has caracul hair
$275.00 each

1954
Wendy-kin Baby, 8"
One-piece vinyl body, hard plastic Little Genius head
Outfit tagged: "Wendy-kin"
$350.00 – 650.00

1957
#205, Little Genius, 8"
Vinyl body, hard plastic head
Organdy dress and bonnet, original booties
$350.00 – 650.00

1956
#743, Little Genius, 8"
Print cotton dress and bonnet
$275.00 – 550.00

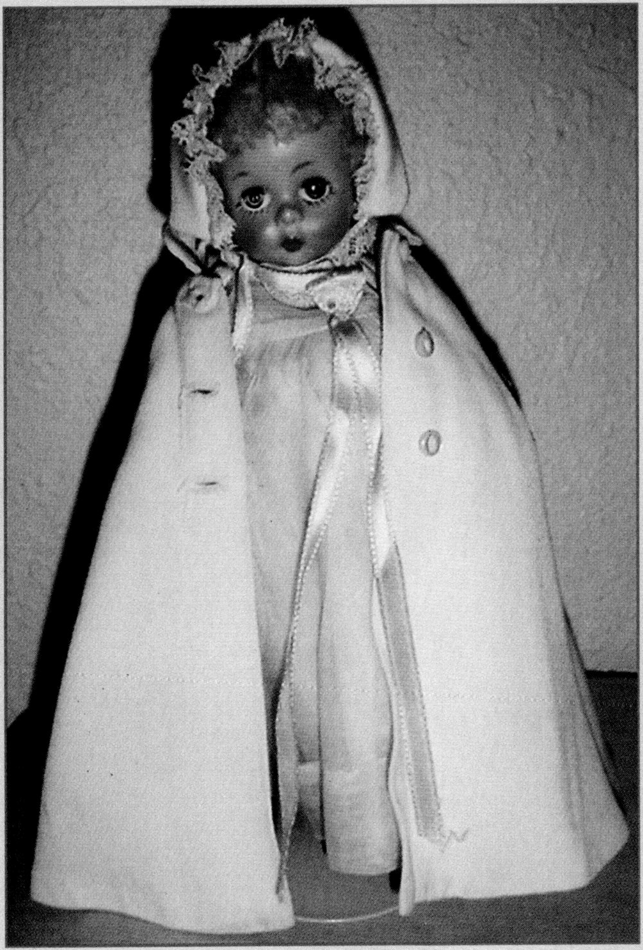

1956
#780, Little Genius, 8"
Vinyl body, hard plastic head, caracul hair
Gabardine coat and hat over organdy dress
$325.00 – 550.00

1956
#756, Little Genius, 8"
Embroidered organdy dress with matching hat
$300.00 – 550.00

Little Genius, 8"
Organdy dress and bonnet with feather stitching around skirt
$275.00 – 500.00

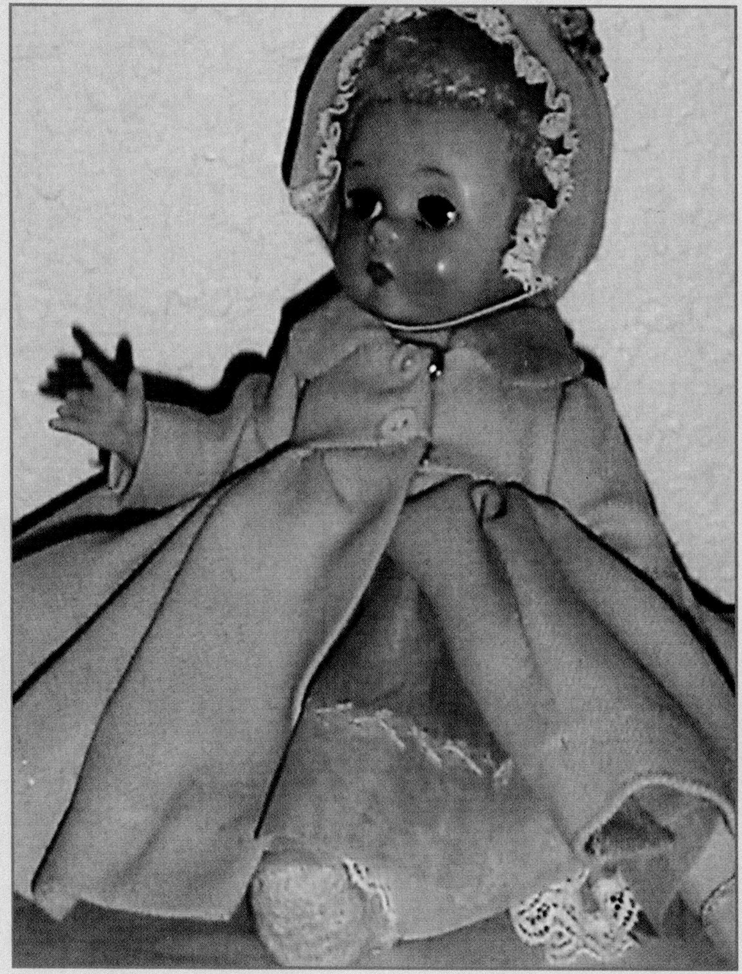

1957
#265, Little Genius, 8"
Flannel coat and hat, velvet collar and trim on hat
$325.00 – 600.00

1961
Little Genius, 8"
Hat and coat are shown on the clothes rack on the 1961 booklet
$275.00 – 550.00

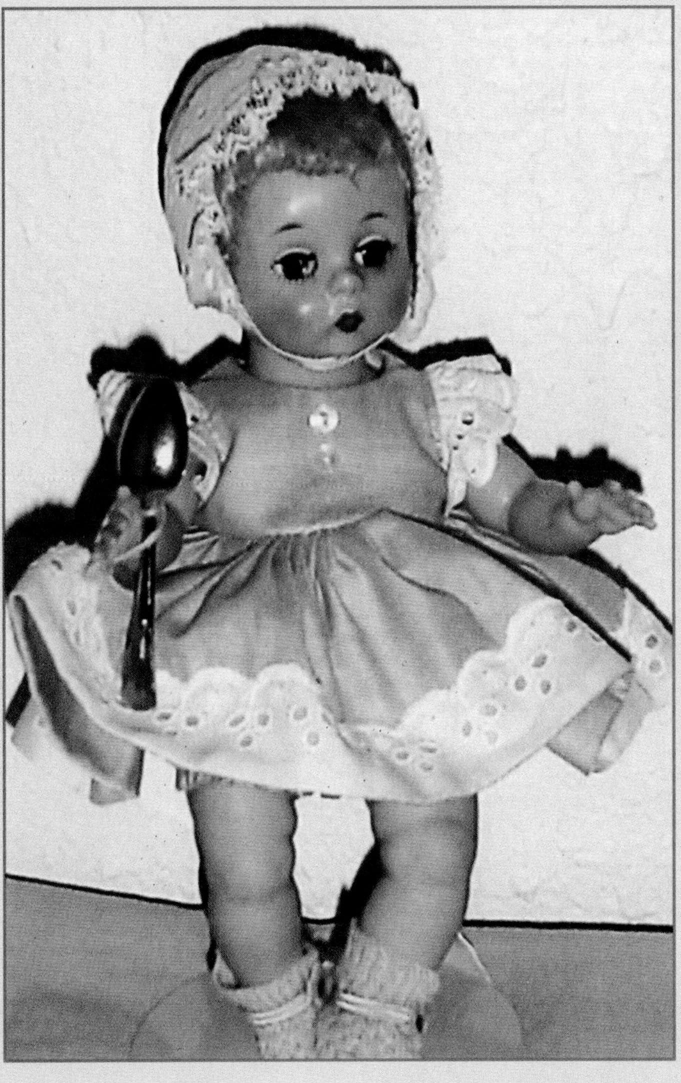

1961
#226, Little Genius, 8"
Polished cotton dress with embroidery, matching hat
Came with spoon
$350.00 – 650.00

Littlest Kitten

Littlest Kitten was made for one year only in 1963. Her body is the jointed vinyl body that is the same as was used on Little Genius. Littlest Kitten's face is more round and is made of vinyl with rooted hair. Her lips do not have the hole to nurse a bottle but her Little Genius body has the hole for wetting. Littlest Kitten is pictured in the 1963 booklet dressed in six outfits and six more outfits are also shown.

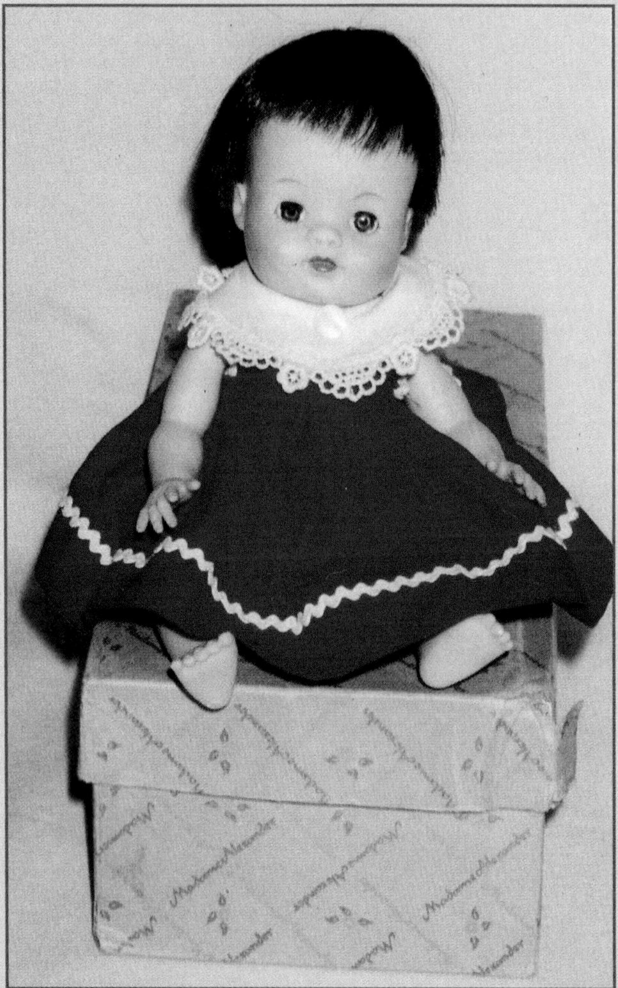

1963
Littlest Kitten, 8"
Vinyl, rooted hair
Original clothes
$250.00 – 475.00

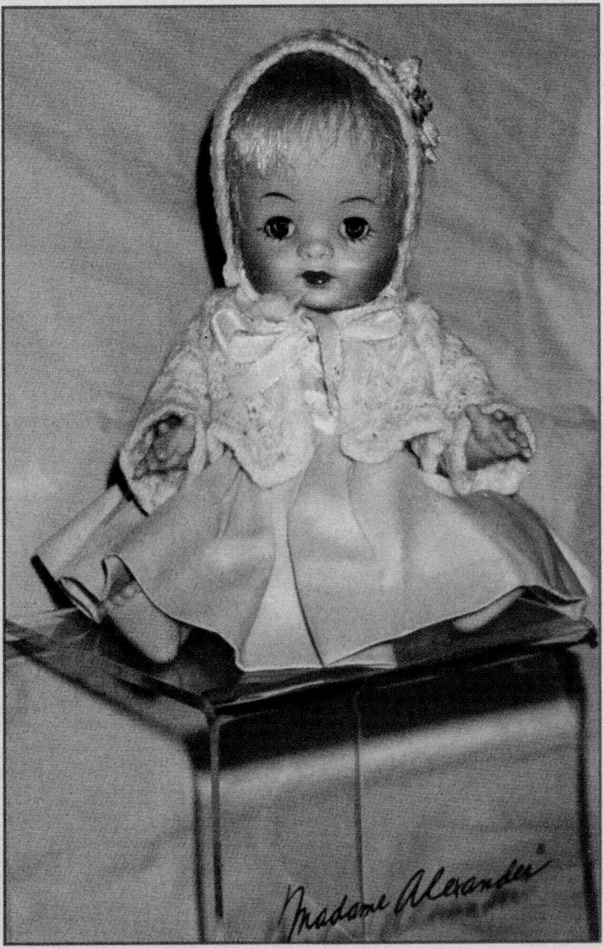

1963
Littlest Kitten, 8"
Vinyl
All original
$275.00 – 500.00

1963
Littlest Kitten, 8"
Original dress and bonnet
$275.00 – 475.00

Maggie was first made in 1949 in hard plastic. The earliest Maggie dolls have a darker complexion while later ones have a creamy complexion. Maggie can be a walker. The Maggie face was used through 1956. Maggie Walker in 1952 is listed as being made in three sizes: 15", 18", and 23". The dolls were marked on the back of the head "Alexander." Maggie was used for many of the dolls in the Little Women sets during these years plus for many other characters including dolls in the Me and My Shadow Series and the Glamour Girls.

1949
Beth of Little Women
(Maggie)
Dress tagged: "Beth"
$450.00 – 800.00

1949
Jo of Little Women, 14"
Hard plastic
(Maggie)
$475.00 – 850.00

1949
Maggie
Original outfit
$325.00

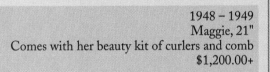

1948 – 1949
Maggie, 21"
Comes with her beauty kit of curlers and comb
$1,200.00+

1950
Alice in Wonderland, 15"
(Maggie)
All original
$475.00+

1950
Maggie dolls
Original dresses
$325.00 each

1951
Alice in Wonderland
(Maggie)
$800.00+

1952
John Powers Model, 14"
(Maggie)
Tag: "John Powers Model"
$1,500.00+

1952
#1810, Annabelle, 18"
(Maggie)
All original
$950.00+

1952
#1815, Maggie Walker, 18"
Referred to as the teenage doll
Comes with her beauty kit
$450.00+

1952
Jo of Little Women, 15"
(Maggie)
$450.00 – 800.00

1953
#2010C, Glamour Girl, 18"
(Maggie)
Pink taffeta skirt with black velvet bodice
$2,200.00+

1953
#2010A, Glamour Girl Godey
(Maggie)
Red taffeta gown and hat, fur cape stole, and red hat box, very rare
$2,300.00+

1950s
Maggie, 14"
Hard plastic walker
Original clothes
$350.00+

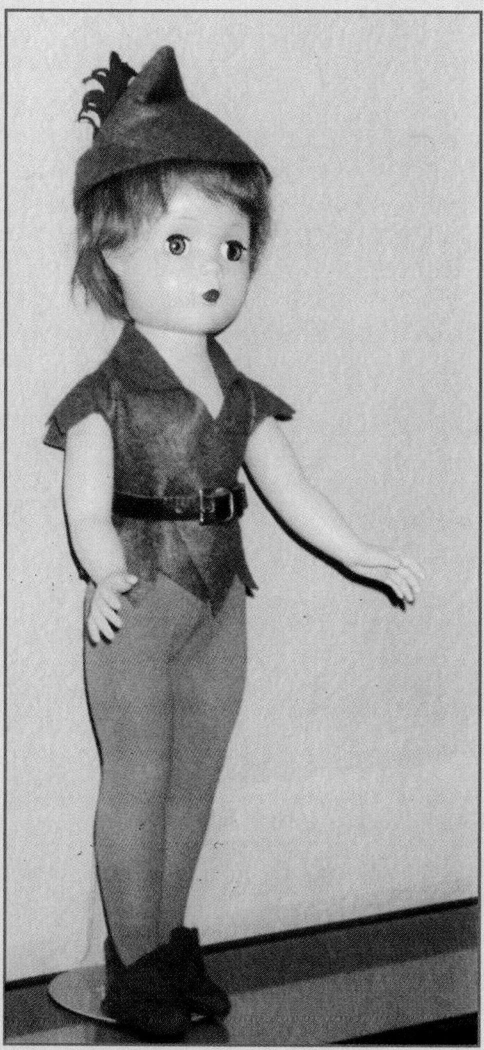

1953
#1505, Peter Pan, 15"
Felt jacket and hat
(Maggie)
$750.00+

1954
2030C, Victoria, 18"
(Maggie)
Taffeta gown with side panniers, hot pink reticule
Me and My Shadow Series
$2,000.00+

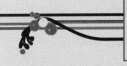

Margaret O'Brien was a child movie star. The first dolls the Alexander Company made of her were made of composition. In 1948, the Margaret face dolls were made of hard plastic. The Margaret face dolls were made until 1956 and the face was used extensively during this period on dozens of different dolls. The Margaret face dolls are marked Alexander on the back of their head, if marked at all. The early dolls had mohair wigs. The 1952 catalog states that all the wigs are loomed and can be washed and set. Cynthia was made with the black Margaret face in 15", 18", and 23" sizes in 1952 and 1953. The Margaret face dolls during this period are some of the highest valued dolls made by Madame Alexander.

1948
McGuffey Ana
(Margaret)
Pink corduroy coat with fur at the collar and cuffs
$2,000.00+

1948
McGuffey Ana, 14"
(Margaret)
$1,200.00+

1948 – 1950
Babs Skaters
(Margaret)
Original costumes
15", $1,200.00+
21", $1,500.00+

1949
Kathryn Grayson, 20"
(Margaret)
Lace and tulle gown, very rare doll
$6,000.00+

1949
Amy of Little Women, 15"
(Margaret)
$700.00+

1949
McGuffey Ana, 14"
(Margaret)
A very beautiful doll
$1,800.00+

1949 – 1951
Nina Ballerina, 14"
Hard plastic
A very hard-to-find doll
$1,500.00+

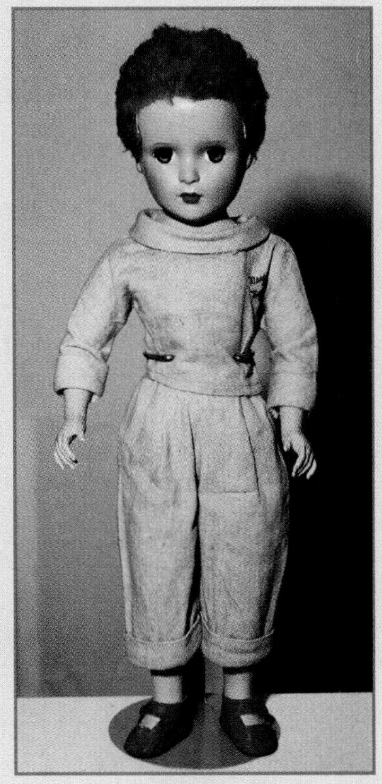

1949 – 1952
(Margaret)
Mary Martin
Jumpsuit with name embroidered on it, caracul wig
$700.00+

1949 – 1951
Nina Ballerina
(Margaret)
Tag in outfit: "Nina Ballerina"
$700.00+

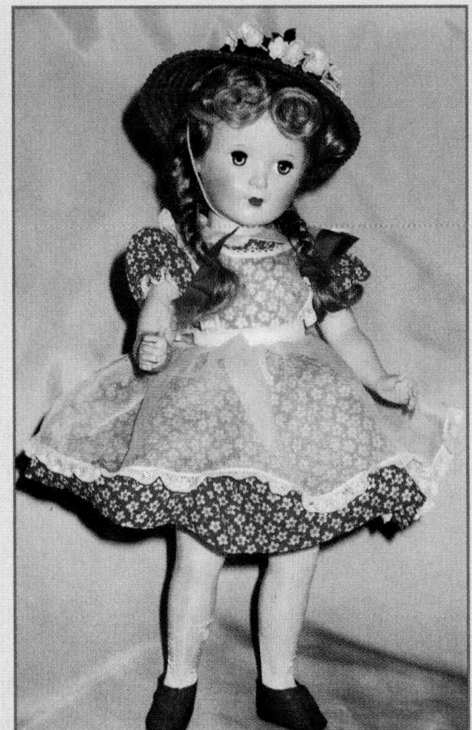

1949
McGuffey Ana, 18"
(Margaret)
All original, hard plastic
$2,000.00+

1950
Godey Lady, 14"
(Margaret)
Pink taffeta dress trimmed in lace
Tag: "Godey Lady"
$1,500.00+

1950
Prince and Cinderella
(Margaret)
Hat is missing on Prince
Prince, $950.00+
Cinderella, $1,000.00+

1950
Margaret Bride, 14"
Mint and all original
$900.00+

Side view of Debra Bride
showing unique bustle.

1950
Debra Bride
(Margaret)
Very unusual gown
with five-piece
layered bustle,
extremely rare doll
$7,500.00+

1949 – 1951
Nina Ballerinas
(Margaret)
All original
$700.00+

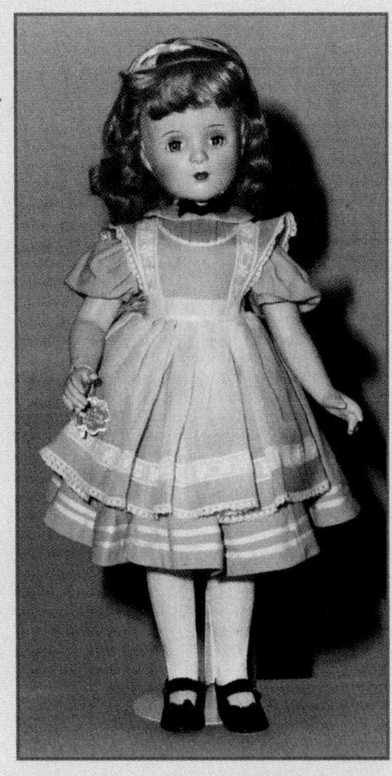

1951 only
Godey, 21"
(Margaret)
Lace and pink satin dress
$1,800.00+

1951
Alice in Wonderland, 18"
(Margaret)
$700.00+

1951
Mystery Dance, 14"
(Margaret)
$4,000.00+

1950 – 1951
Poor Cinderella, 14"
Hard plastic
$700.00+

1952 only
#1835, Snow White, 18"
(Margaret)
All original
$1,000.00+

1951
Fashions of the Century Bride, 18"
(Margaret)
Two coiled braids, tagged and all original, extremely rare doll
$3,000.00+

1952
#1850, Bride
Lace trimmed satin gown
with rhinestones on bodice
$1,000.00+

1952
#1500, Meg of Little Women, 15"
(Margaret)
$450.00 – 800.00

1953
#2020A, Queen Elizabeth II, one of seven 18" Glamour Girls
(Margaret)
Court gown of brocade with the blue sash of the garter
$1,800.00+

1953
#1852, Wendy Bride
(Margaret)
Walker, original hat box
$1,800.00+

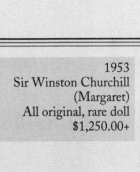

1953
Sir Winston Churchill
(Margaret)
All original, rare doll
$1,250.00+

1953
#2001A, Picnic Day, 18"
Glamour Girl
(Margaret)
Pink print gown, catalog reprint states she is ready for a garden party
$2,000.00+

1953
#2001C, Edwardian
Glamour Girl
(Margaret)
Strawberry pink gown trimmed in val lace
$2,400.00+

1953
#2001B
Glamour Girl
Party gown of blue with tiny rosebuds trimmed with val lace, white straw hat trimmed with roses.
$2,400.00+

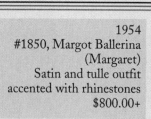

1954
#1850, Margot Ballerina
(Margaret)
Satin and tulle outfit accented with rhinestones
$800.00+

Mary Ann

14" Mary Ann face was only made in 1965. Her head and arms were made of vinyl while the rest of her body was made of plastic. Mary Ann was made with three outfits in 1965. The doll was also made as Orphan Annie and in an Orphan Annie window box gift set with extra clothes in 1965. The Mary Ann doll has been used for a large part of the Alexander line for over thirty years.

1965
Mary Ellen Playmate, 14"
(Mary Ann)
Red cotton dress with white eyelet, made for Marshall Fields
$275.00 – 400.00

1965
Alice and Her Party Kit, 14"
Made exclusively for FAO Schwarz
Came with extra outfits and accessories
$750.00

Melinda was made in 1962 and 1963 only. The smiling face is molded with painted upper teeth. The head and arms are vinyl while the body and legs are plastic. The head is marked "Alexander 1962." She was made in 14", 16", and 22" sizes. In 1962, the 18" Bunny was made with the same head but a slightly different body. Melinda has a swivel waist on the 16" and 22" sizes. A Kelly face Melinda was made in the 20" and 23" sizes in 1963.

1963
#1410, Melinda, 14"
Nylon tulle tutu trimmed with flowers and rhinestones, plastic/vinyl doll
$325.00 – 475.00

1963
Left: #1620, Melinda, 16"
Organdy with lace dress
Right: #1612, Melinda, 16"
Checked cotton dress
Both have swivel waists
$250.00 – 400.00 each

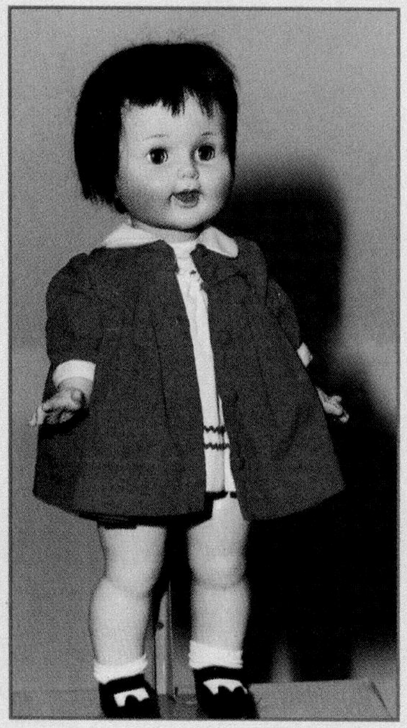

1962
#1820, Bunny, 18"
Plastic/vinyl, dress and coat set, missing bonnet
$250.00 – 375.00

Marybel

Marybel was made from 1959 to 1965. Madame Alexander made "Marybel, the doll that gets well" in 1959 as a gift to be purchased for sick children. The 16" doll had rooted hair and was made of rigid vinyl. She had a swivel waist and brown eyes. The doll wore a pink satin romper and came with leg and arm casts, crutches, sunglasses, spots for measles and chicken pox, and bandages.

The Marybel face was also used for Edith, the Lonely Doll, Elise, Kelly, Pollyanna, and the Queen in 1961.

Country Cousin

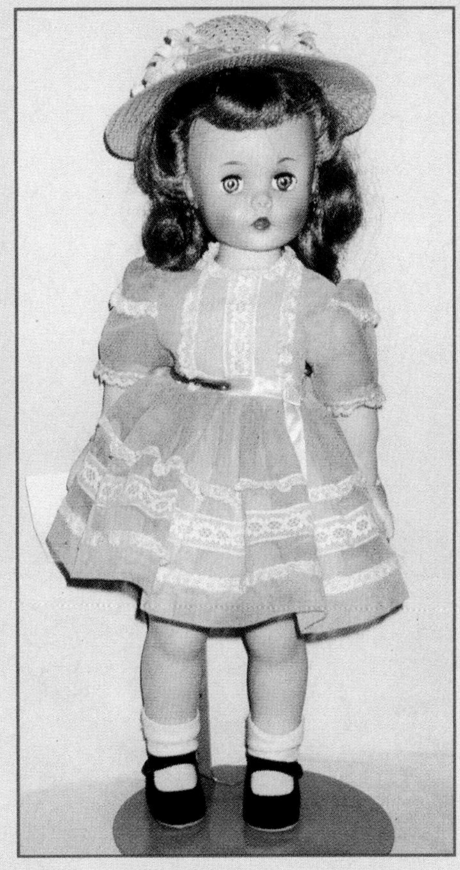

1958
#1912, Kelly, 22"
(Marybel)
Nylon party dress trimmed in val lace
$375.00 – 525.00

1958
Country Cousin, 16"
(Marybel)
Cotton print dress and straw hat with flowers
$350.00 – 500.00

1959
#1650, Edith the Lonely Doll, 16"
(Marybel)
From Dare Wright's books
Checked dress with apron
$350.00 – 575.00

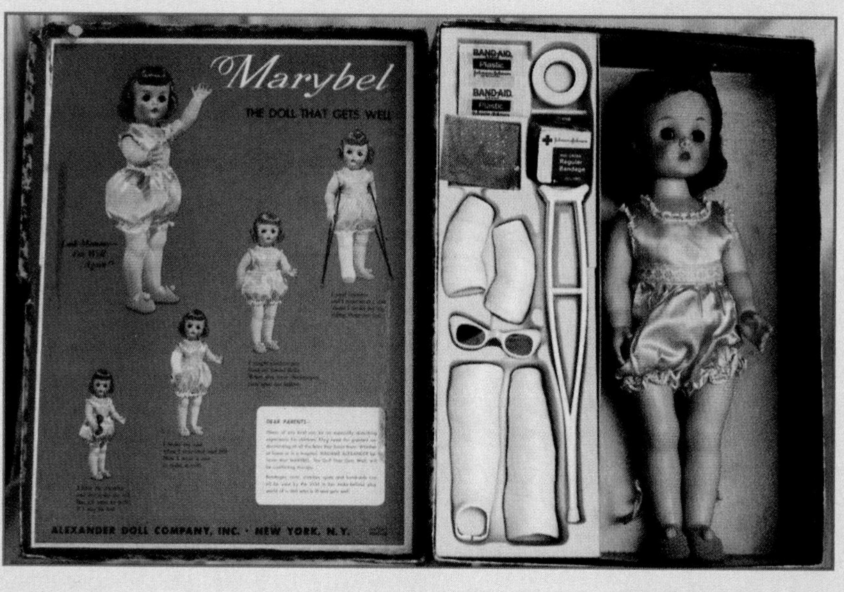

1959
#1670, Marybel the Doll That Gets Well, 16"
(Marybel)
Was made to give to children when ill
$325.00

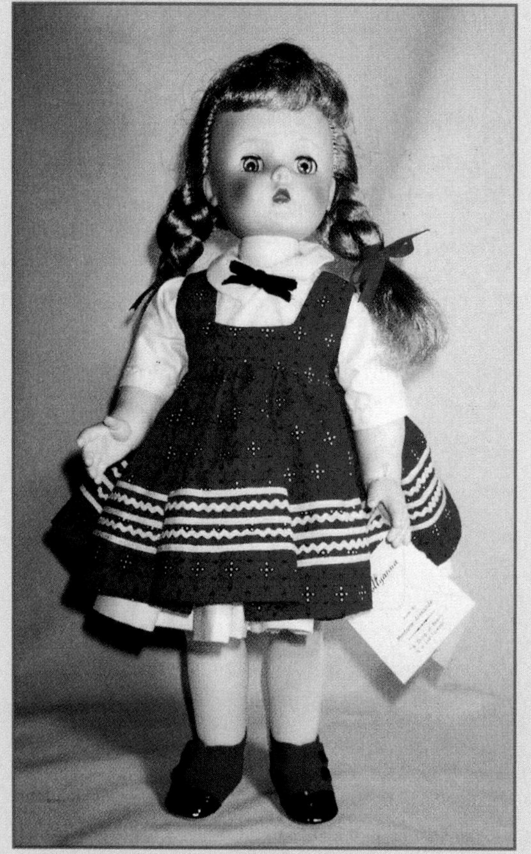

1960
#1531, Pollyanna, 16"
(Marybel)
Polished cotton dress with pinafore, high button shoes
$375.00 – 550.00

Polly

The 17" Polly doll was made in 1965 only. She was made of plastic and vinyl with long thin arms and legs. Ten different outfits were made for Polly in 1965 including evening gowns, street dresses, bride gowns, and a ballerina outfit. The Polly face was used also for Leslie, Maria, large set of *The Sound of Music*, Molly and Marlo Thomas.

1965
#1751, Polly, 17"
Mauve tulle formal
$375.00 – 550.00

1965
#1725, Polly, 17"
Pink tulle with sequin bodice
$275.00 – 450.00

1965
#1651, Leslie, 17"
Vinyl/plastic, sequin decorated bodice with pleated tulle skirt
$325.00 – 575.00

Smarty

Smarty, 12", was made in 1962 and 1963 in a toddler body of plastic and vinyl. She had rooted hair and was made as a dressed doll in several outfits, but extra clothes also could be purchased separately. The Smarty face was also used for Kate, a black doll.

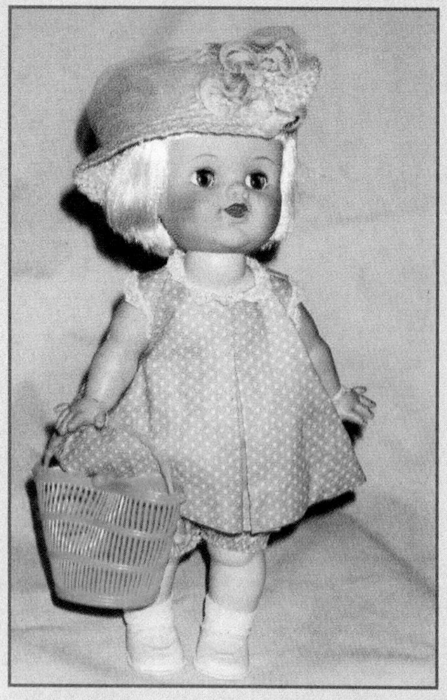

1962
#1140, Smarty, 12"
Vinyl head with rooted hair, pink cotton dress with white dots, all original
$275.00 – 500.00

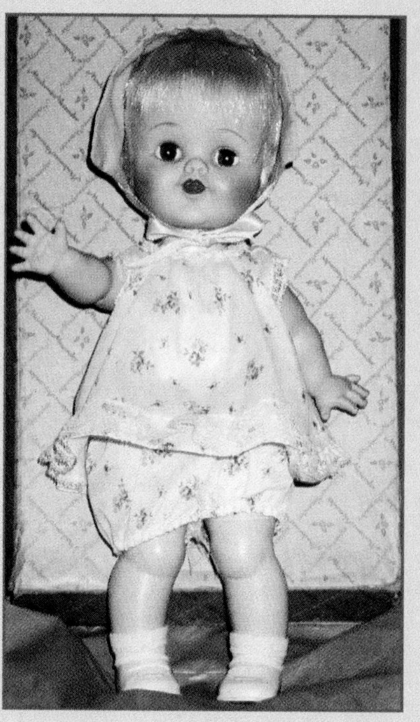

1962
#1136, Smarty, 12"
Plastic/vinyl, original clothes
$250.00 – 475.00

1962
#1141, Smarty
Cute cotton outfit, all original
$300.00 – 500.00

1963 only
#1136, 12", Katie
Yellow dress trimmed in lace with yellow sash at waist
$325.00 – 550.00

Miscellaneous

sThrough the years Madame Alexander has offered a variety of items for purchase other than dolls. Some of the items were made at the factory and some were not, but sold under the Alexander license. One example is the tea set that was made in Germany in 1962. It was marked Germany but was sold in the square Alexander window box that so many of the extra outfits were sold in. Madame sold furniture, clothes racks, wooden and metal tables and chairs, beds, and vanities. Pictured are the wonderful poodles from the 1950s and the beautiful bedding set.

1956
#30
Flower print pillows and sheets for 8" to 10" dolls in original box
$150.00

1950s
#80
Velveteen sofa with gold braid, original cushions, made for 8" to 10" dolls
$275.00

1950s
#64
Velveteen chair with gold braid for 8" to 10" dolls
$100.00

1954
Mr. and Mrs. Inky, 14"
Boy and girl poodles
$475.00+ each

Early 1950s
French poodle
Dark gray with black flecks
Won a blue ribbon at a Madame Alexander convention
$1,100.00+

Back of gray and black poodle

About the Author

Linda C. Crowsey is the author of nine *Madame Alexander Collector's Dolls Price Guides*, volumes 22 through 30. She is also the author of *Madame Alexander Store Exclusives and Limited Editions*, published in 2000. She began collecting Madame Alexander dolls in 1975 and is a thirty year member of the Madame Alexander Doll Club. Ms. Crowsey served six years on the MADC Board of Directors and served as vice president of MADC for two years. She has written articles for *The Review* as well as other publications. She often gives lectures and slide presentations on Madame Alexander dolls to clubs and at doll events. Ms. Crowsey is a charter member of Who's Who in MADC and was presented the Hart Award at the 2005 San Jose MADC Convention for her years of work for the Madame Alexander Doll Club.

Linda and her husband, Howard, celebrated their fortieth wedding anniversary in 2004. They have three children and six grandchildren.

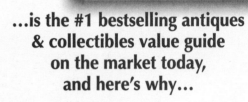